ellen forney

ROCK STEADY

Brilliant Advice FROM MY Bipolar Life

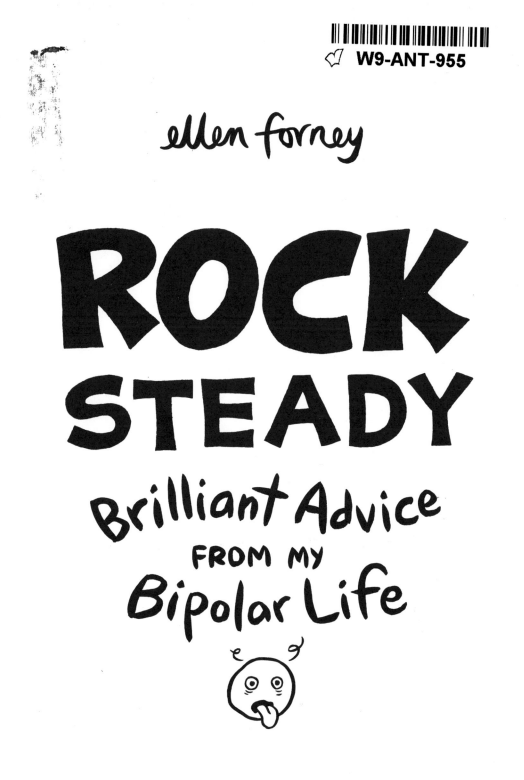

FANTAGRAPHICS BOOKS INC.
7563 Lake City Way NE
Seattle, Washington, 98115

Editor and Associate Publisher: Eric Reynolds
Book Design: Ellen Forney and Keeli McCarthy
Production: Paul Baresh
Editorial assistance: RJ Casey, Avi Kool,
and Kristy Valenti
Publisher: Gary Groth

ISBN 978-1-68396-101-7
Library of Congress Control Number: 2017957014

First printing: May 2018
Printed in China

CONTENTS

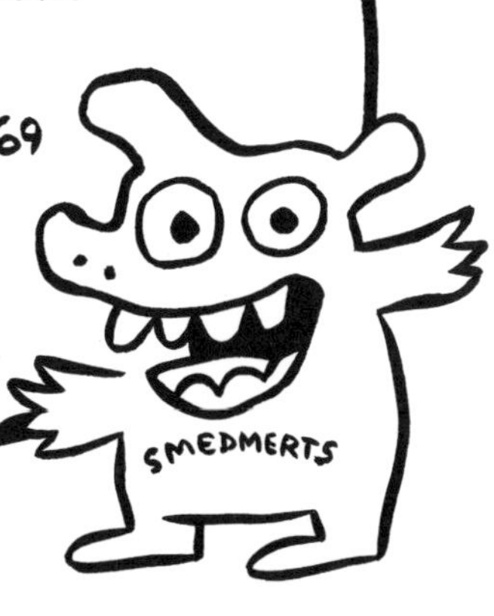

SMEDMERTS

INTRODUCTION

Hi! I'm Ellen Forney, bipolar cartoonist.

I WAS DIAGNOSED WITH BIPOLAR DISORDER IN 1998, SHORTLY BEFORE MY 30TH BIRTHDAY. I WAS IN A VERY MANIC SWING AT THE TIME, THEN FELL INTO A DEEP DEPRESSION, THEN STRUGGLED FOR FOUR YEARS TO GET STABLE.

MARBLES: MANIA, DEPRESSION, MICHELANGELO, & ME IS MY GRAPHIC MEMOIR ABOUT THAT TIME. I ALSO INCLUDED SOME OF THE COPING TOOLS I FOUND ALONG THE WAY.

MARBLES

SINCE MARBLES CAME OUT IN 2012, I'VE HEARD FROM SO MANY PEOPLE WITH MOOD DISORDERS WHO WERE THANKFUL FOR THE INFORMATION & COMPANY. SO I DECIDED TO WRITE THIS FOLLOW-UP BOOK WITH A FLIPPED FOCUS: MOSTLY COPING TOOLS, WITH MY PERSONAL POINT OF VIEW.

HERE WE ARE! WELCOME!

GETTING STABLE IS REALLY TOUGH. MAINTAINING STABILITY OVER THE LONG TERM IS A WHOLE OTHER CHALLENGE. IDEALLY, IT'S LESS DRAMATIC, BUT IT'S JUST AS DEMANDING.

I FIGURED I'D BE WRITING WITH THE CERTAINTY OF FOURTEEN YEARS OF EPISODE-FREE WISDOM-COLLECTING. BUT WHATEVER WISDOM I HAVE INCLUDES KNOWING THAT THE ONLY CONSTANT IS CHANGE, & THAT THE TASK OF MAINTAINING STABILITY IS NEVER A DONE DEAL.

A FEW MONTHS INTO STARTING ROCK STEADY...

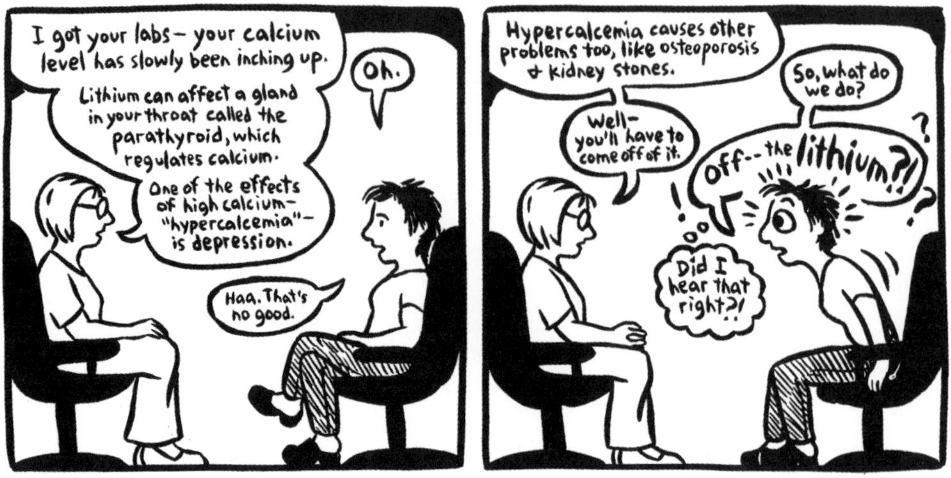
I got your labs— your calcium level has slowly been inching up.
Lithium can affect a gland in your throat called the parathyroid, which regulates calcium.
One of the effects of high calcium— "hypercalcemia"— is depression.
Oh.
Haa. That's no good.
Hypercalcemia causes other problems too, like osteoporosis & kidney stones.
So, what do we do?
Well— you'll have to come off of it.
off-- the lithium?!
Did I hear that right?!

LITHIUM HAS BEEN ONE OF MY TWO MOOD STABILIZERS FOR THOSE FOURTEEN YEARS. THE OTHER, LAMOTRIGINE, ISN'T ENOUGH ON ITS OWN. KAREN'S NEWS THREW ME INTO A TAILSPIN.

I TURNED TO MY MOM & MY PARTNER FOR SUPPORT. I LOOKED UP OXCARBAZEPINE, THE MOOD STABILIZER KAREN SUGGESTED WE TRY NEXT. I WROTE & DREW IN MY JOURNAL.

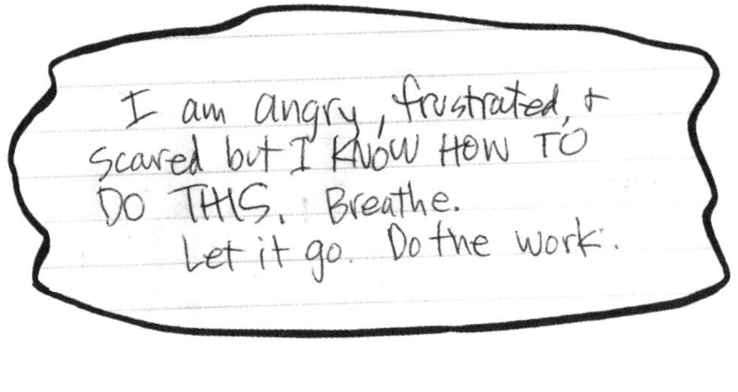
I am angry, frustrated, & scared but I KNOW HOW TO DO THIS. Breathe. Let it go. Do the work.

I RESENTED OXCARBAZEPINE. I DREW A STUPID OX IN A STUPID CAR.

I WANTED TO GET ORGANIZED & BE EXTRA DILIGENT ABOUT TAKING CARE OF MYSELF. I WANTED A **STABILITY MAINTENANCE GUIDE.** AND LO, HERE I WAS, ALREADY WRITING ONE.

SO STRANGE.

SO I'VE GOTTEN A PERSONAL TEST RUN. I'VE LEARNED A TON.

ROCK STEADY IS FOCUSED ON BIPOLAR DISORDER, BUT IS ALSO FOR ANY MOOD DISTURBANCE — TOOLS TO COMFORT OURSELVES, RECOGNIZE DANGER SIGNS, & JUST LIVE WITH A GOOD DEAL OF UNCERTAINTY & CRAZINESS.

THIS BOOK IS FOR YOU, FOR ME, & FOR ANYONE SEEKING BALANCE IN HANDLING THE UPS & DOWNS, THE CRISES & ANNOYANCES, & FOR JUST LEARNING HOW TO ROCK STEADY.

CHAPTER 1 BASICS

WHAT, WHERE, WHEN??

TAKING CARE OF YOURSELF & YOUR MOODS CAN MEAN ANYTHING FROM MAINTAINING AN ARRAY OF ROUTINE HABITS & COPING TOOLS TO NAVIGATING A DISARRAY OF CRISES, UNPREDICTABLE SETBACKS, & INEVITABLE STUMBLES.

WHETHER YOU'RE MAINTAINING STABILITY OR WORKING YOUR WAY TOWARD IT, YOU HAVE SOME KEY THINGS TO STAY ON TOP OF, SOME **KEY KEY** THINGS TO STAY ON TOP OF, & A LOT OF OPTIONS & CHOICES.

THE **KEY, KEY** THINGS TO STAY ON TOP OF ARE:

GET ENOUGH SLEEP,

& IF MEDS ARE PART OF YOUR TREATMENT, **TAKE YOUR MEDS.**

OTHER KEY THINGS ARE:

EAT WELL,

SEE YOUR **DOCTOR** & STICK TO YOUR THERAPY,

HAVE A **MINDFULNESS** * **MEDITATION** PRACTICE,

EXERCISE REGULARLY,

HAVE A PRETTY REGULAR **ROUTINE,**

AN ARRAY OF **COPING TOOLS,**

& A SOLID **SUPPORT SYSTEM.**

DIFFERENT MENTAL HEALTH PHILOSOPHIES HAVE DIFFERENT EMPHASES. MANY HAVE CATCHY MNEMONICS!

"SNAP"!*
SLEEP
NUTRITION
ACTIVITY
PEOPLE

"THE FOUR S'S"!**
STRUCTURE
STRESS
SLEEP
SELF-MONITOR

MY OWN MENTAL HEALTH PHILOSOPHY IS THAT SELF-CARE ENTAILS A WIDE, INTERLOCKING, LIFE-SPANNING RANGE OF ESSENTIALS. AND THUS,

THE ROCK STEADY STRATEGY IS:

SLEEP
MEDS
EAT
DOCTOR
MINDFULNESS
EXERCISE
ROUTINE
TOOLS
SUPPORT SYSTEM

SMEDMERTS!

PLUS WE HAVE A MASCOT!

*PREVENTING BIPOLAR RELAPSE, BY DR. RUTH WHITE (NEW HARBINGER, 2014)
**FACING BIPOLAR, BY DR. RUSS FEDERMAN & DR. J.A. THOMPSON (NEW HARBINGER, 2010)

GET ENOUGH ① SLEEP

GOOD SLEEP IS OUR TOP PRIORITY. WE NEED IT FOR PRETTY MUCH EVERY MIND & BODY FUNCTION, COGNITIVE & PHYSICAL.

OUR MOODS, ALREADY OFF-KILTER, GET THROWN OFF EVEN MORE BY LACK OF SLEEP, OR EVEN JUST BY CHANGES IN OUR SLEEP PATTERNS (LIKE DAYLIGHT SAVINGS OR JET LAG).

DECREASED SLEEP IS A SYMPTOM OF A MOOD DISORDER, BUT INADEQUATE SLEEP BY ITSELF CAN CAUSE OR KICK IN A PERCOLATING MOOD SWING.

AN AVERAGE GOOD NIGHT'S SLEEP IS 7-9 HOURS.

BUT, SHOW OF HANDS:  INSOMNIA ANYONE??

YES, SLEEP DISTURBANCE IS CRUELLY COMMON WITH MOOD DISORDERS.

MANY TOOLS FOR GETTING A GOOD NIGHT'S SLEEP IN CHAPTER 3!

IF MEDS ARE PART OF YOUR TREATMENT,
② TAKE YOUR MEDS...

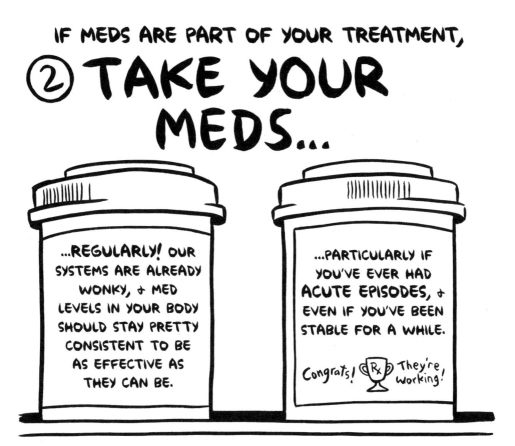

...REGULARLY! OUR SYSTEMS ARE ALREADY WONKY, & MED LEVELS IN YOUR BODY SHOULD STAY PRETTY CONSISTENT TO BE AS EFFECTIVE AS THEY CAN BE.

...PARTICULARLY IF YOU'VE EVER HAD **ACUTE EPISODES,** & EVEN IF YOU'VE BEEN STABLE FOR A WHILE.

Congrats! They're working!

...WITH WHATEVER **PLAN** YOU WORKED OUT WITH YOUR DOCTOR.

IF FOR ANY REASON YOU **DON'T WANT TO TAKE** YOUR MEDS, TELL YOUR DOCTOR & WORK OUT A NEW PLAN TO SWITCH MEDS OR TAPER DOWN OR OFF. STOPPING ON YOUR OWN IS A HUGE RISK FOR KICKING IN A NEW EPISODE.

MANY TOOLS TO MAKE TAKING PILLS LESS OF A DRAG IN CHAPTER 4.

③ EAT WELL

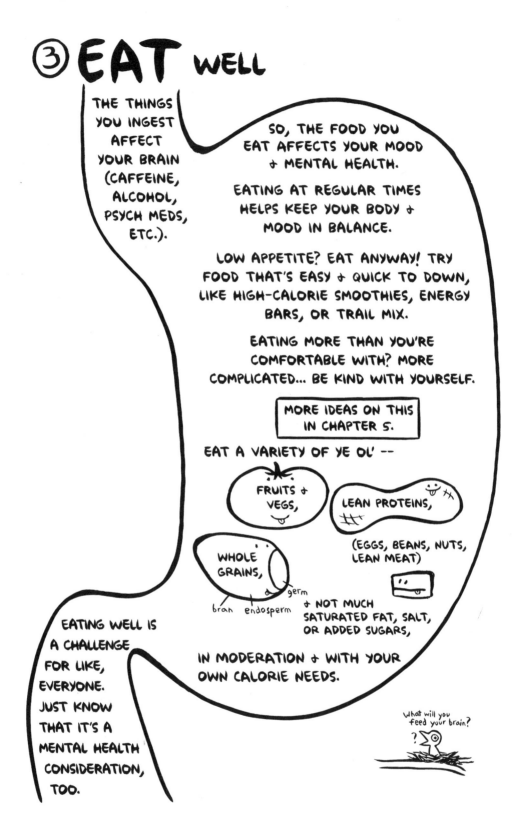

THE THINGS YOU INGEST AFFECT YOUR BRAIN (CAFFEINE, ALCOHOL, PSYCH MEDS, ETC.).

SO, THE FOOD YOU EAT AFFECTS YOUR MOOD & MENTAL HEALTH.

EATING AT REGULAR TIMES HELPS KEEP YOUR BODY & MOOD IN BALANCE.

LOW APPETITE? EAT ANYWAY! TRY FOOD THAT'S EASY & QUICK TO DOWN, LIKE HIGH-CALORIE SMOOTHIES, ENERGY BARS, OR TRAIL MIX.

EATING MORE THAN YOU'RE COMFORTABLE WITH? MORE COMPLICATED... BE KIND WITH YOURSELF.

MORE IDEAS ON THIS IN CHAPTER 5.

EAT A VARIETY OF YE OL' --

FRUITS & VEGS,

LEAN PROTEINS,

(EGGS, BEANS, NUTS, LEAN MEAT)

WHOLE GRAINS,

bran endosperm germ

& NOT MUCH SATURATED FAT, SALT, OR ADDED SUGARS,

IN MODERATION & WITH YOUR OWN CALORIE NEEDS.

EATING WELL IS A CHALLENGE FOR LIKE, EVERYONE. JUST KNOW THAT IT'S A MENTAL HEALTH CONSIDERATION, TOO.

What will you feed your brain?

?

④ SEE YOUR DOCTOR

BY "DOCTOR" I MEAN YOUR PROFESSIONAL TREATMENT PERSON OR TEAM — PSYCHIATRIST, PSYCHOLOGIST, COUNSELOR. YOU NEED TO HAVE A KNOWLEDGEABLE DOCTOR THAT YOU TRUST, & EFFECTIVE TREATMENT THAT YOU CAN STICK WITH.

- CALL YOUR DOCTOR IF SOMETHING'S WEIRD
- OR WORRISOME
- OR IN AN EMERGENCY
- OR IF YOU'RE HAVING SIDE EFFECTS

- ASK YOUR DOCTOR QUESTIONS ABOUT MOOD DISORDERS
- & TREATMENT OPTIONS
- TELL YOUR DOCTOR IF THINGS ARE TOUGH
- GET KNOWLEDGEABLE SUPPORT
- & GUIDANCE WITH MEDICATIONS

YOUR DOCTOR IS YOUR MECHANIC, YOUR GPS, & YOUR TOW TRUCK DRIVER WHEN YOU'RE STUCK IN A DITCH.

SHE HAS THE TOOLS & TRAINING TO KEEP YOU RUNNING EVEN WHEN SHE'S NOT AROUND.

> MORE ON FINDING A DOCTOR IN CHAPTER 2.

PRACTICE
⑤ MEDITATION *
MINDFULNESS

THIS PRACTICE INVOLVES BRINGING YOUR AWARENESS TO THE PRESENT MOMENT, WITHOUT JUDGMENT, & QUIETING YOUR BUSY BRAIN (EVEN JUST FOR SPLIT SECONDS).

e.g. listening to a sound without deeming it "good" or "bad"

IT'S PRACTICING BEING IN THE MOMENT WHILE STAYING STILL FOR A PERIOD OF TIME ("MEDITATION" IS MORE ABOUT THIS PART)...

breath
breath
breath
colors
textures
breeze

...AND BEING IN THE MOMENT IN THE WORLD ("MINDFULNESS" IS MORE ABOUT THIS PART).

SOME OF THE MANY MENTAL HEALTH BENEFITS:

- LEARNING TO CALM YOURSELF & LOWER YOUR STRESS LEVEL, OVERALL & IN SPECIFIC SITUATIONS THAT CAN SET OFF AN EMOTIONAL SPIRAL (ANYTHING FROM MINOR ANNOYANCES & FRUSTRATIONS, TO BIG FEARS & GRIEF).

- IMPROVING SLEEP IN GENERAL & AS PART OF RELAXATION TECHNIQUES FOR INSOMNIA.

- HELPING TO SLOW DOWN OR STOP OBSESSING OR RUMINATING ON THINGS THAT UPSET YOU.

TECHNIQUES & IDEAS IN CHAPTER 3.

GET REGULAR ⑥ EXERCISE

A FEW TIMES A WEEK. SOMETHING THAT GETS YOUR HEART RATE UP A BIT. RHYTHMIC EXERCISES LIKE WALKING, RUNNING, OR SWIMMING ARE GREAT. YOGA IS FABULOUS. FIND SOMETHING YOU ENJOY.

phoo   phoo   phoo   phoo

EXERCISE ACTIVATES THE BRAIN'S ANXIETY-RELIEVING NEUROTRANSMITTERS, SUPPORTS OVERALL PHYSICAL HEALTH, INVITES A SENSE OF WELL-BEING & COMFORT IN YOUR BODY, & HELPS REGULATE YOUR EATING.

IN OTHER WORDS: FEELS GOOD, IS GOOD.

WATCH IT IF YOU'RE MANIC OR SENSING AN ONCOMING EPISODE, THOUGH. SUPER-HARD WORKOUTS & MANIA ARE LINKED & CAN FEED ON EACH OTHERS' HIGH ENERGY.

What!   endorphins   That's when I want to work out hard! No fair!   CORRECT!

JUST LIKE "EAT WELL," THIS IS WAY EASIER SAID THAN DONE, BUT HERE AGAIN, KNOW IT'S A CONSIDERATION FOR YOUR MENTAL HEALTH, TOO.

IDEAS ON IR-REGULAR EXERCISE IN CHAPTER 3.

KEEP A REGULAR
⑦ ROUTINE

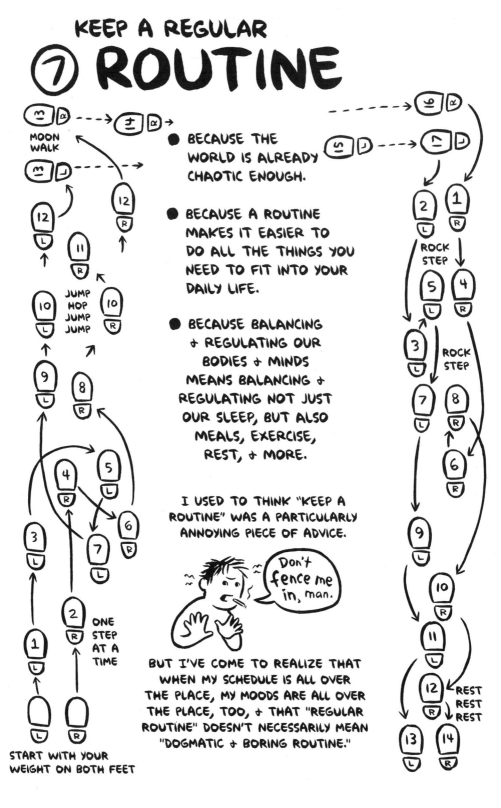

MOON WALK

BECAUSE THE WORLD IS ALREADY CHAOTIC ENOUGH.

BECAUSE A ROUTINE MAKES IT EASIER TO DO ALL THE THINGS YOU NEED TO FIT INTO YOUR DAILY LIFE.

BECAUSE BALANCING & REGULATING OUR BODIES & MINDS MEANS BALANCING & REGULATING NOT JUST OUR SLEEP, BUT ALSO MEALS, EXERCISE, REST, & MORE.

I USED TO THINK "KEEP A ROUTINE" WAS A PARTICULARLY ANNOYING PIECE OF ADVICE.

Don't fence me in, man.

JUMP HOP JUMP JUMP

ONE STEP AT A TIME

START WITH YOUR WEIGHT ON BOTH FEET

BUT I'VE COME TO REALIZE THAT WHEN MY SCHEDULE IS ALL OVER THE PLACE, MY MOODS ARE ALL OVER THE PLACE, TOO, & THAT "REGULAR ROUTINE" DOESN'T NECESSARILY MEAN "DOGMATIC & BORING ROUTINE."

ROCK STEP

ROCK STEP

REST REST REST

KEEPING A REGULAR ROUTINE GOES HAND IN HAND WITH BEING ATTUNED TO YOUR CIRCADIAN RHYTHMS.

CIRCADIAN RHYTHMS ARE OUR BIOLOGICAL CLOCK – PHYSICAL, MENTAL, & BEHAVIORAL CHANGES THAT FOLLOW A ROUGHLY 24-HOUR CYCLE.

"CIRCA-DIAN"
LATIN: ABOUT A DAY

OUR MASTER CLOCK IS IN OUR BRAIN. IT'S CONNECTED TO OUR RETINA & RESPONDS TO LIGHT.

ALMOST EVERY CELL IN OUR BODY HAS A CLOCK THAT WORKS WITH THE MASTER CLOCK.

ALMOST ALL ANIMALS
& PLANTS
& FUNGI
& SOME BACTERIA
FUNCTION ON THIS DAILY CYCLE.

Be regular & orderly in your life, so that you may be violent & original in your work.

GUSTAVE "FLUFFY" FLAUBERT

BIPOLAR DISORDER IS LINKED TO AN OFF-RHYTHM BODY CLOCK, WHICH CAN SET EVERYTHING ELSE OFF – HENCE THE NEED FOR AN EXTRA-DELIBERATELY MAINTAINED ROUTINE.

HAVE PLENTY OF
⑧ COPING TOOLS

HABITS, RESOURCES, INFORMATION, & PROBLEM-SOLVING STRATEGIES...

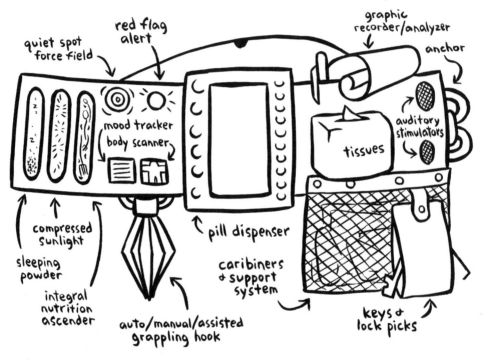

...FROM BOOKS, ARTICLES, FRIENDS, DOCTORS...

& ADAPTATIONS OF THOSE, & THINGS YOU MAKE UP YOURSELF...

...THINGS FOR MAINTAINING THE BASICS, RECALIBRATING YOUR MOODS, RECOGNIZING DANGER ZONES, DEALING WITH EPISODES & CRISES, & JUST KEEPING A SENSE OF YOURSELF.

THE MORE TOOLS YOU HAVE, THE MORE SITUATIONS YOU CAN HANDLE, & THE MORE YOU CAN MIX & MATCH & FORMULATE NEW FIXES FOR THE PREDICTABLE & UNPREDICTABLE BUMPS IN THE FUTURE.

⑨ HAVE A SOLID EMOTIONAL & LOGISTICAL SUPPORT SYSTEM

GATHER YOUR TEAM – PEOPLE WHO CARE ABOUT YOU & KNOW YOU HAVE A MOOD DISORDER. LISTEN TO THEM WHEN THEY'RE CONCERNED, & REACH OUT TO THEM WHEN YOU COULD USE SOME HELP.

BESIDES YOUR **DOCTOR,**

See you then.

Call me if you need to.

YOUR SUPPORT TEAM MIGHT INCLUDE--

FAMILY

Love you!

I'm listening.

SOMEONE TO NOTICE WHEN YOUR ENERGY IS UNUSUALLY HIGH OR LOW

A SHOULDER TO CRY ON

I looked up that article for you.

FRIENDS

SOMEONE THAT'LL CALL IN THE MORNINGS TO SAY "I LOVE YOU," EVEN WHEN THAT'S HARD TO BELIEVE.

A SAFETY NET

I'll be over with popcorn & a warm puppy who adores you!

It's okay.

Come have dinner with us!

COMMUNITY

Got your message- I'll pick you up at 3!

SOMEONE YOU DON'T HAVE TO EXPLAIN YOURSELF TO WHEN YOU'RE FEELING OUT OF WHACK

SOMEONE TO TAKE YOU TO THE E.R.

TAKING CARE OF OUR MOOD DISORDERS IS TOO MUCH TO DO ALL BY OURSELVES. IT JUST IS.

HERE'S MY OWN SMEDMERTS SYSTEM:

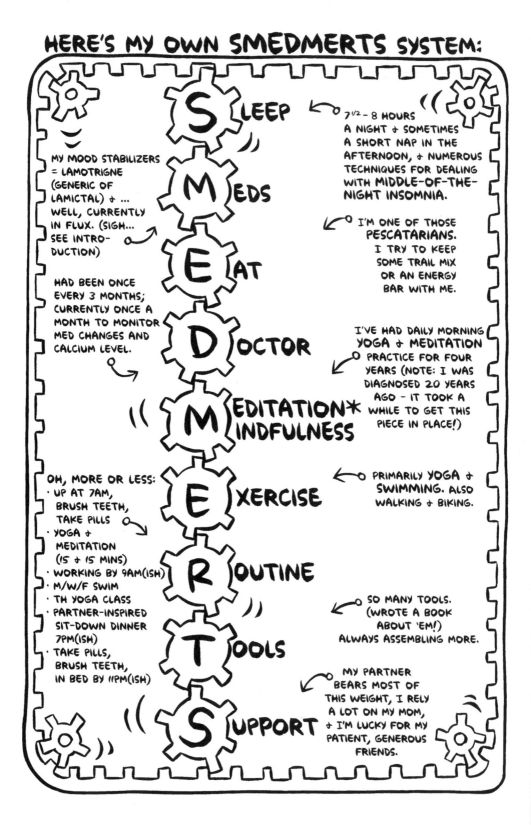

SLEEP — 7½ – 8 HOURS A NIGHT & SOMETIMES A SHORT NAP IN THE AFTERNOON, & NUMEROUS TECHNIQUES FOR DEALING WITH MIDDLE-OF-THE-NIGHT INSOMNIA.

MY MOOD STABILIZERS = LAMOTRIGNE (GENERIC OF LAMICTAL) & ... WELL, CURRENTLY IN FLUX. (SIGH... SEE INTRO-DUCTION)

MEDS

EAT — I'M ONE OF THOSE PESCATARIANS. I TRY TO KEEP SOME TRAIL MIX OR AN ENERGY BAR WITH ME.

HAD BEEN ONCE EVERY 3 MONTHS; CURRENTLY ONCE A MONTH TO MONITOR MED CHANGES AND CALCIUM LEVEL.

DOCTOR

MEDITATION* & MINDFULNESS — I'VE HAD DAILY MORNING YOGA & MEDITATION PRACTICE FOR FOUR YEARS (NOTE: I WAS DIAGNOSED 20 YEARS AGO – IT TOOK A WHILE TO GET THIS PIECE IN PLACE!)

OH, MORE OR LESS:
· UP AT 7AM, BRUSH TEETH, TAKE PILLS
· YOGA & MEDITATION (15 & 15 MINS)
· WORKING BY 9AM(ISH)
· M/W/F SWIM
· TH YOGA CLASS
· PARTNER-INSPIRED SIT-DOWN DINNER 7PM(ISH)
· TAKE PILLS, BRUSH TEETH, IN BED BY 11PM(ISH)

EXERCISE — PRIMARILY YOGA & SWIMMING. ALSO WALKING & BIKING.

ROUTINE

TOOLS — SO MANY TOOLS. (WROTE A BOOK ABOUT 'EM!) ALWAYS ASSEMBLING MORE.

SUPPORT — MY PARTNER BEARS MOST OF THIS WEIGHT, I RELY A LOT ON MY MOM, & I'M LUCKY FOR MY PATIENT, GENEROUS FRIENDS.

WHAT IS STABILITY, ANYWAY?

STABILITY IS **ACTIVE**. BETWEEN LIFE, THE UNIVERSE, & THE WILY NATURE OF MOOD DISORDERS, THINGS ARE CONSTANTLY SHIFTING. STABILITY MEANS FIGURING OUT HOW TO--

FIND BALANCE...

GETTING OFF THE ROLLER COASTER WITH EFFECTIVE TREATMENTS & MINDSETS & BEHAVIORS...

& MAINTAIN BALANCE,

WITH A SELF-AWARE LIFE OF CALIBRATING & RECALIBRATING.

SOME OF THE BIGGEST **CHALLENGES** TO STABILITY INCLUDE--

-- NOT TO MENTION ISSUES AROUND ACCESS TO HEALTH CARE & COSTS & DEALING WITH STIGMA, & EVEN JUST THE TIME & ENERGY IT TAKES TO EXERCISE **AND** SLEEP ENOUGH & TO GO TO THERAPY AND EVERYTHING ELSE.

STABILITY MEANS FIGURING OUT HOW TO PRIORITIZE WHAT SERVES YOU, NOT FEELING LIKE A FAILURE IF YOU DON'T DO EVERYTHING PERFECTLY, & JUST BALANCING EVERYTHING AS BEST YOU CAN.

BECAUSE:

 YOUR BODY WILL BE HEALTHIER.

 YOU'LL BE BETTER ABLE TO KEEP RELATIONSHIPS THAT ARE IMPORTANT TO YOU.

 YOU MAY AVOID OUT-OF-CONTROL MANIA & ROCK-BOTTOM DEPRESSION...

 ...AND EACH EPISODE MAKES YOU MORE SUCEPTIBLE TO FUTURE EPISODES, HOSPITALIZATION, SUICIDAL THOUGHTS, & ALL THAT.

 IT TURNS OUT TAKING CARE OF YOURSELF IS PRETTY GREAT.

 BECAUSE YOU'RE A STAR, & BECAUSE YOU DESERVE IT.

STABILITY IS A **LIFELONG** PROJECT FOR ANYONE WITH A MOOD DISORDER.

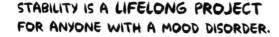

IT GETS EASIER!

BUT IT TAKES COMMITMENT.

BE SURE TO GIVE YOURSELF PLENTY OF CREDIT.

MERIT BADGES

FOR COMMITTING TO TAKING CARE OF YOURSELF

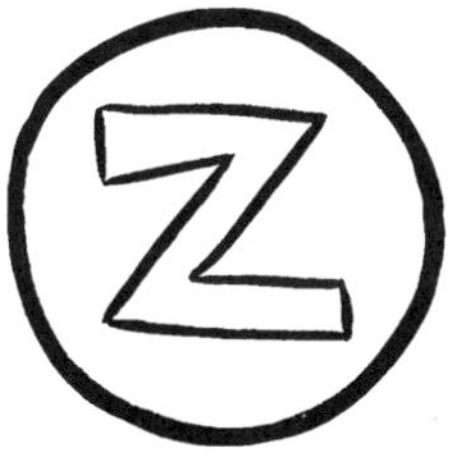

SLEEP

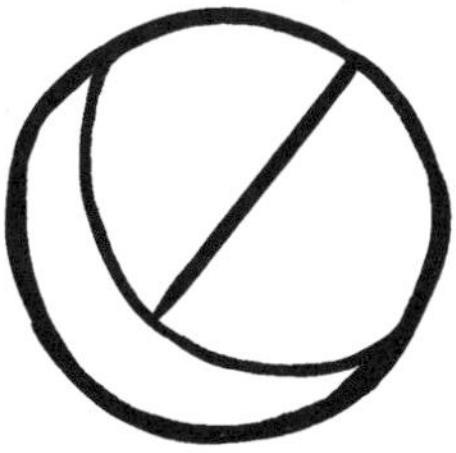

MEDS

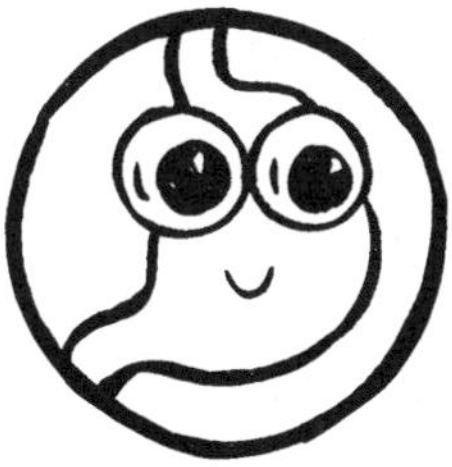

EAT

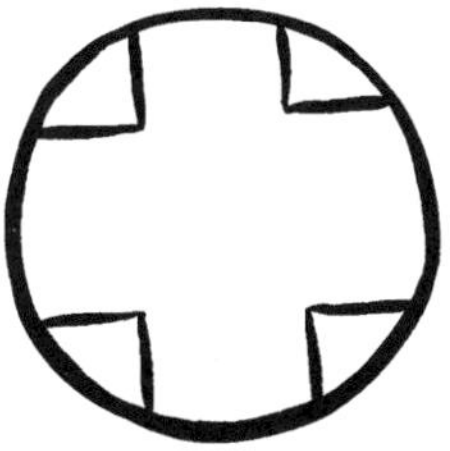

DOCTOR & TREATMENT

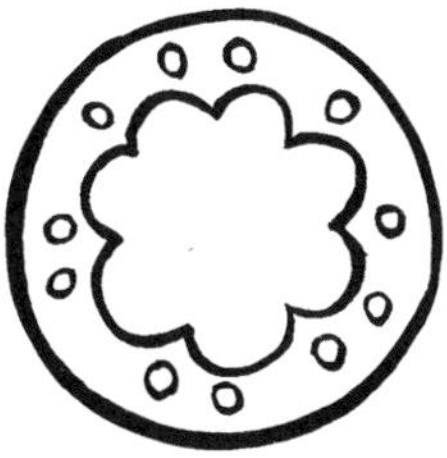

MINDFULNESS

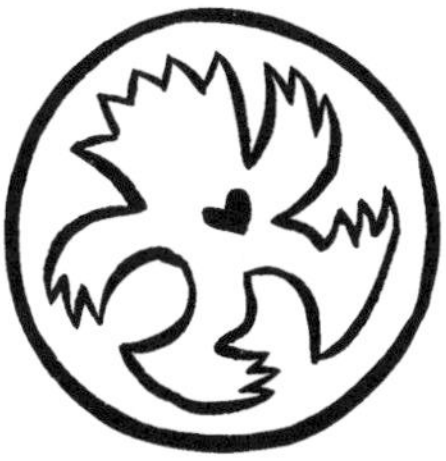

EXERCISE

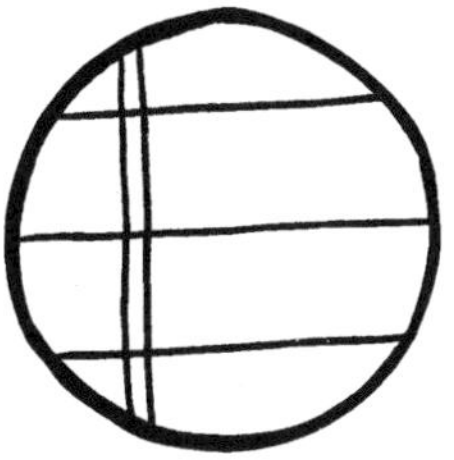

ROUTINE

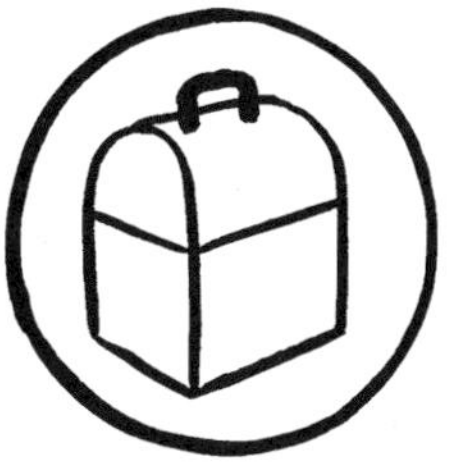

COPING TOOLS

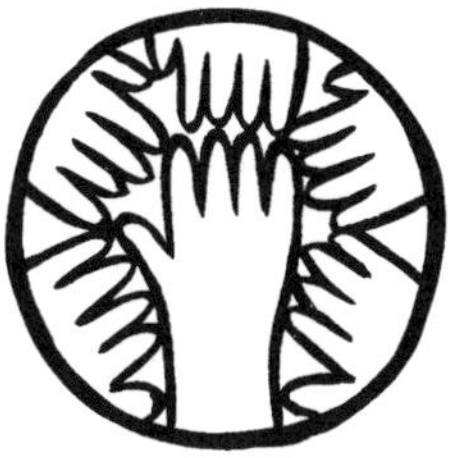

SUPPORT SYSTEM

TAKE THE PLEDGE:

"I'M NOT ALONE,
THINGS GET BETTER & WORSE,
I CAN DO IT.
SMEDMERTS!"

(& KISS THE BACK OF YOUR OWN HAND FOR SELF-APPRECIATION & RESPECT)

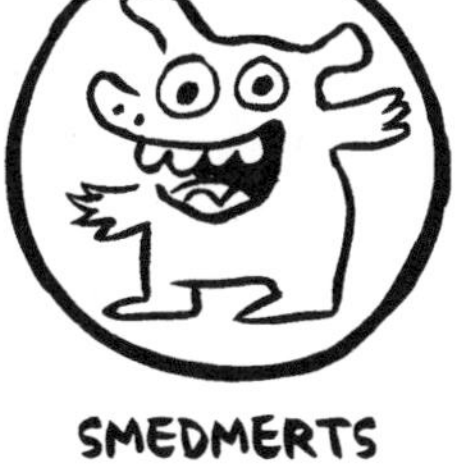

SMEDMERTS

CHAPTER 2
THERAPY

THERE ARE MANY APPROACHES TO MENTAL HEALTH CARE.
IT'S TRICKY TO FIND THE RIGHT ONE(S) FOR YOU.

CHOOSING A THERAPY MAY FEEL THIS RANDOM, BUT NEED NOT BE THIS RANDOM.

THE ULTIMATE GOALS ARE TO **STABILIZE** IN THE SHORT TERM
♦ **STAY STABLE** FOR THE LONG TERM,
WITH TREATMENT FOR YOUR

MIND   BODY   ♦ ENVIRONMENT.

♠   ♡   ♣   ◇

E.G.
DEALING WITH STRESS
RECOGNIZING RED FLAGS
SELF-AWARENESS

E.G.
MEDS
SLEEP
EXERCISE

E.G.
RELATIONSHIPS
SEASONS
RESOURCES

WHERE TO START? WHAT ARE SOME **OPTIONS?**

EVERYONE'S SYMPTOMS ARE A LITTLE DIFFERENT. YOUR TREATMENT
NEEDS TO ADDRESS THE PARTICULAR WAYS YOUR DISORDER AFFECTS **YOU.**

BIPOLAR DISORDER & MAJOR DEPRESSION ARE UNDER THE UMBRELLA OF

MOOD DISORDERS,

CONDITIONS WHERE EMOTIONS ARE DERAILED FOR
EXTENDED PERIODS OF TIME. THE MAIN TYPES ARE:

☆ **BIPOLAR I:** ←(that's me)
   ALTERNATING MANIC & DEPRESSIVE EPISODES

☆ **BIPOLAR II:**
   ALTERNATING HYPOMANIC & DEPRESSIVE EPISODES
   ↖"HYPOMANIA" = MILD MANIA

☆ **CYCLOTHYMIA:**
   ALTERNATING HYPOMANIC & MILD DEPRESSIVE EPISODES

☆ **UNIPOLAR DEPRESSION:**
   SINGLE OR RECURRENT EPISODES WITH NO MANIA

☆ **DYSTHYMIA:**
   CHRONIC, LOW-GRADE DEPRESSION

...WHICH REFER TO THESE **MOOD STATES:**

MANIA	HYPO-MANIA	MIXED STATES	RAPID CYCLING	EUTHYMIA	DYSTHYMIA	MILD DEPRESSION	DEPRESSION
UP UP up! up! up	up!	up↓down at the same time	4 or more episodes within 12 weeks	balanced, "normal"	chronically low	low	low low low low low

NOTE: SOME BIPOLAR PEOPLE EXPERIENCE MANIA AS HIGH ENERGY
BUT NOT EUPHORIC. FEELING **"DYSPHORIC"** MIGHT MEAN AMPED BUT
IRRITABLE, EASILY MOVED TO ANGER, OR IMPATIENT.

ANOTHER NOTE: "BIPOLAR DISORDER" & "MANIC DEPRESSION" ARE THE SAME THING.

SYMPTOMS & TRAITS OF MOOD DISORDERS

AS DEFINED IN THE DSM, THE OFFICIAL (IF CONTROVERSIAL) PSYCHIATRIC USER'S MANUAL SINCE 1952.

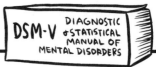

MANIC EPISODE
MORE THAN ONE WEEK OF SIGNIFICANT--

◇ HIGHER ENERGY

◇ DECREASED SLEEP

◇ TALKATIVENESS

◇ RACING THOUGHTS

◇ DISTRACTIBILITY

◇ MAKING BIG PLANS

◇ LOTS OF SEXUAL ENERGY

ALSO...

◇ OVERSPENDING

◇ MAKING RASH DECISIONS THAT IMPACT RELATIONSHIPS, WORK, &/OR SOCIAL LIFE

◇ LOOSER BOUNDARIES

◇ WILD SELF-CONFIDENCE

DEPRESSIVE EPISODE
MORE THAN TWO WEEKS OF SIGNIFICANT--

● DEPRESSED MOOD MOST OF THE TIME

● DECREASED INTEREST IN ACTIVITIES THAT HAD BEEN PLEASURABLE

● WEIGHT GAIN -OR- LOSS

● SLEEPING MORE -OR- LESS

● FIDGETY -OR- SLUGGISH

● TIRED

● FEELING WORTHLESS & VULNERABLE

● INABILITY TO CONCENTRATE

● THINKING ABOUT DEATH

ALSO...

● ISOLATING SELF

● IRRITATION

● RESTLESSNESS

● ANHEDONIA

A GREAT WORD FOR A TERRIBLE FEELING: "INABILITY TO FEEL PLEASURE." (THE GREEK ROOT, "HEDON," MEANS "PLEASURE" - AS IN "HEDONISM," BUT LIKE, SO NOT HEDONISM.

VERY DIFFERENT EXPERIENCES, BUT, I'D SAY THERE'S SOME **SIGNIFICANT OVERLAP**: ANXIETY, BRAIN FEELING FRIED, FEELING OUT OF CONTROL, GETTING DISCONNECTED FROM FAMILY & OLD FRIENDS.

ANOTHER ASPECT OF MOOD DISORDERS IS THAT WE **CYCLE** THROUGH OUR MOOD STATES. BECAUSE WE HAVE A RANGE OF MOODS, IT MEANS WE NEED TO HANDLE UPS, DOWNS, MIDDLES, & THE SWINGS BETWEEN THEM. FOR EXAMPLE, THIS IS A COMMON BIPOLAR 1 PATTERN:

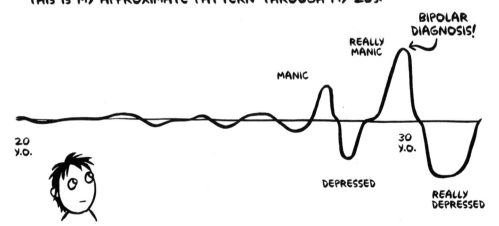

THE PATTERNS ARE DIFFERENT FOR DIFFERENT PEOPLE & AT DIFFERENT TIMES — HOW HIGH, HOW LOW, HOW FREQUENT, ETC.

THIS IS MY APPROXIMATE PATTERN THROUGH MY 20S:

SOMETIMES I'M ASKED IF I WISH I'D BEEN DIAGNOSED IN MY TEENS OR EARLY 20S. BUT I DON'T THINK I REALLY HAD A **DISORDER** THEN. INCREASING STRETCHES OF HIGHER OR LOWER MOOD, BUT WITHIN NORMAL RANGE — NOT ACUTE ENOUGH TO DISORDER THINGS UNTIL MY LATE 20S.

WHAT ABOUT MISDIAGNOSIS?

A GOOD DIAGNOSIS IS IMPORTANT SO YOU CAN MAP OUT A TREATMENT PLAN THAT SUITS YOU & THAT YOU FEEL CONFIDENT COMMITTING TO.

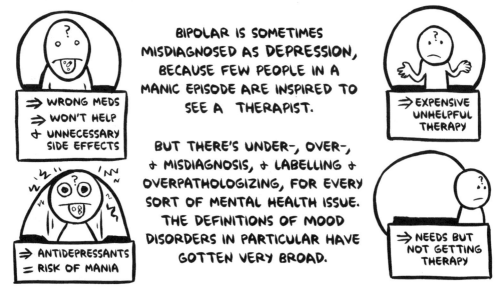

BIPOLAR IS SOMETIMES MISDIAGNOSED AS DEPRESSION, BECAUSE FEW PEOPLE IN A MANIC EPISODE ARE INSPIRED TO SEE A THERAPIST.

BUT THERE'S UNDER-, OVER-, & MISDIAGNOSIS, & LABELLING & OVERPATHOLOGIZING, FOR EVERY SORT OF MENTAL HEALTH ISSUE. THE DEFINITIONS OF MOOD DISORDERS IN PARTICULAR HAVE GOTTEN VERY BROAD.

⇒ WRONG MEDS
⇒ WON'T HELP
& UNNECESSARY SIDE EFFECTS

⇒ ANTIDEPRESSANTS = RISK OF MANIA

⇒ EXPENSIVE UNHELPFUL THERAPY

⇒ NEEDS BUT NOT GETTING THERAPY

A DIAGNOSIS SHOULD COME FROM A KNOWLEDGEABLE MENTAL HEALTH SPECIALIST. YOUR BRAIN IS AN INCREDIBLY COMPLEX & LITTLE-UNDERSTOOD ORGAN, & THERE ARE NO SIMPLE TESTS TO TELL WHAT'S WHAT.

ASK YOURSELF:

DID THE DOCTOR SPEND A GOOD AMOUNT OF TIME WITH ME BEFORE MAKING A DIAGNOSIS?

DO THEY KNOW WHAT'S GOING ON WITH ME PHYSICALLY & IN MY LIFE?

DID THEY ASK ABOUT MY FAMILY HISTORY?

DID THEY ASK ABOUT MY OWN HISTORY?

THE MAIN TWO SYMPTOMS OF MANIA ARE HIGH ENERGY & LACK OF SLEEP. DOES THAT DESCRIBE ME?

DOES THIS DIAGNOSIS JUST... FEEL RIGHT?

IF YOU'RE NOT SURE, GET A SECOND OPINION. FIND A DOCTOR YOU TRUST!

OF THE MANY KINDS OF MENTAL HEALTH PROFESSIONALS, WHO DO YOU LOOK FOR? HERE ARE YOUR MAIN CHOICES.

PSYCHIATRIST — MD DO

MEDICAL DOCTOR SPECIALIZING IN ILLNESS OF THE BRAIN — SOME DO TALK THERAPY BUT MOST ONLY PRESCRIBE & ADJUST MEDS.

PSYCHOLOGIST — PHD PSYD EDD MS

SPECIALIST IN ILLNESS OF THE BRAIN — DOES TALK THERAPY & COPING SKILLS, BUT DOESN'T PRESCRIBE MEDS.

PRIMARY CARE DOCTOR — MD DO

A GENERAL PRACTITIONER CAN CHECK IF YOUR SYMPTOMS ARE RELATED TO SOME OTHER PHYSICAL ILLNESS, REFER YOU TO A THERAPIST, & PRESCRIBE MEDS.

SOCIAL WORKER — DSW MSW LCSW LICSW CCSW

COUNSELOR — MA MS LMFT MFCC MFT LPC LCPC

THERAPISTS FROM A WIDE VARITY OF TRAINING BACKGROUNDS OFFER TALK THERAPY & COPING SKILLS RELATED TO THOUGHTS & ACTION.

PSYCHIATRIC NURSE — APRN PMHN

MEDICAL NURSE SPECIALIZING IN MENTAL HEALTH — CAN HELP WITH TREATMENT PLANS & COUNSELING.

SOME HAVE ADDITIONAL SPECIALIZED TRAINING, E.G. IN DIALECTICAL BEHAVIOR THERAPY (DBT) OR COGNITIVE BEHAVIORAL THERAPY (CBT).

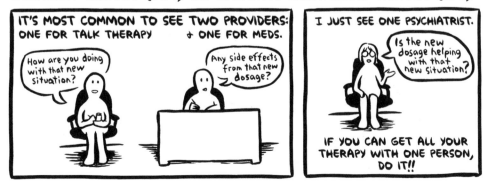

HOW TO FIND YOUR MENTAL HEALTH PROFESSIONAL

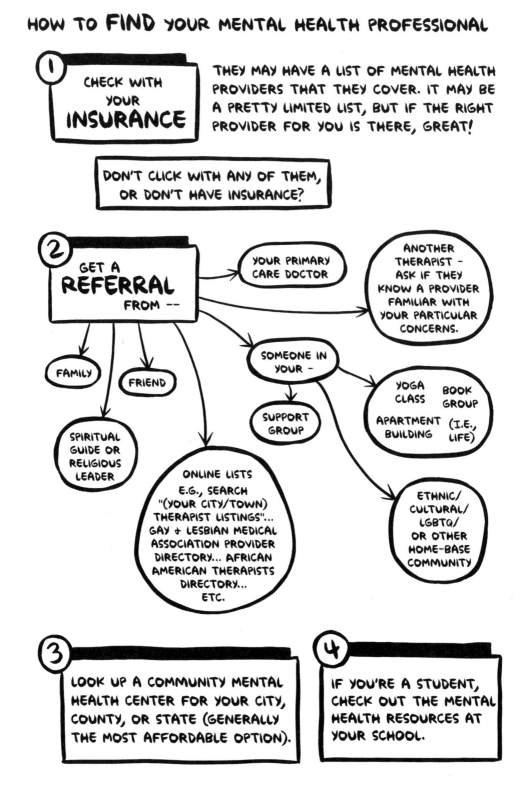

① CHECK WITH YOUR INSURANCE

THEY MAY HAVE A LIST OF MENTAL HEALTH PROVIDERS THAT THEY COVER. IT MAY BE A PRETTY LIMITED LIST, BUT IF THE RIGHT PROVIDER FOR YOU IS THERE, GREAT!

DON'T CLICK WITH ANY OF THEM, OR DON'T HAVE INSURANCE?

② GET A REFERRAL FROM --

- YOUR PRIMARY CARE DOCTOR
- ANOTHER THERAPIST - ASK IF THEY KNOW A PROVIDER FAMILIAR WITH YOUR PARTICULAR CONCERNS.
- FAMILY
- FRIEND
- SPIRITUAL GUIDE OR RELIGIOUS LEADER
- ONLINE LISTS E.G., SEARCH "(YOUR CITY/TOWN) THERAPIST LISTINGS"... GAY & LESBIAN MEDICAL ASSOCIATION PROVIDER DIRECTORY... AFRICAN AMERICAN THERAPISTS DIRECTORY... ETC.
- SOMEONE IN YOUR -
  - SUPPORT GROUP
  - YOGA CLASS   BOOK GROUP
  - APARTMENT BUILDING   (I.E., LIFE)
  - ETHNIC/ CULTURAL/ LGBTQ/ OR OTHER HOME-BASE COMMUNITY

③ LOOK UP A COMMUNITY MENTAL HEALTH CENTER FOR YOUR CITY, COUNTY, OR STATE (GENERALLY THE MOST AFFORDABLE OPTION).

④ IF YOU'RE A STUDENT, CHECK OUT THE MENTAL HEALTH RESOURCES AT YOUR SCHOOL.

THERE ARE ADDED HURDLES TO FINDING MENTAL HEALTH CARE IN NON-WHITE COMMUNITIES. SEATTLE'S SOMALI HEALTH BOARD DESCRIBES MENTAL HEALTH ISSUES AMONG SOMALI IMMIGRANTS & REFUGEES:

The concept of therapy is almost unknown to the Somali community.

The Somali language doesn't even have words for different mental illnesses. Either you are Wa'alan — insane & running down the street naked — or you are sane.

Most Somalis just distrust Western treatments in general. Most turn to Quran reading & prayer.

Men are ashamed to admit emotional crises. Any need for care is seen as a sign of weakness.

& IMRAN

HANA ABDI MOHAMED   AHMED ALI
SOMALI HEALTH BOARD, SEATTLE

MANY CULTURES OF COLOR HAVE SIMILAR ISSUES, INVOLVING SOCIAL EXPECTATIONS OF INDEPENDENCE & STRENGTH, MISCONCEPTIONS ABOUT MENTAL ILLNESS, TURNING MAINLY TO RELIGION FOR HEALING, & LACK OF ACCESS TO CULTURALLY APPROPRIATE CARE. (ONLY A SMALL PERCENTAGE OF THERAPISTS ARE NON-WHITE OR OPENLY NON-STRAIGHT.)

THEIR ADVICE,
IF YOUR FAMILY OR COMMUNITY ISN'T SUPPORTIVE--

KNOW THAT YOUR ILLNESS IS NOT A WEAKNESS.

REACH OUT TO PEOPLE YOU TRUST.	LOOK FOR RESOURCES OUTSIDE YOUR USUAL SUPPORT SYSTEM.
FIND A CULTURALLY APPROPRIATE THERAPIST. THEY MAY NOT BE EASY TO FIND BUT THEY'RE OUT THERE.	TAKE CARE OF YOURSELF. YOU KNOW YOUR BODY BEST.

EVERYONE RESPONDS DIFFERENTLY TO DIFFERENT TREATMENTS. WHAT WORKS FOR YOU MAY BE CLEAR RIGHT AWAY, OR IT MAY TAKE A LONG TIME. SHORT-TERM SOLUTIONS MAY BE DIFFERENT FROM LONG-TERM.

HERE'S A BRIEF OVERVIEW OF THE MOST ESTABLISHED

THERAPIES.

NOTE: TREATMENT FOR BIPOLAR & DEPRESSION HAVE OVERLAPS & IMPORTANT DIFFERENCES.

PSYCHOTHERAPY

TALK THERAPY

MEDICATION

FOR THE BIOLOGICAL ASPECTS OF ILLNESS

COGNITIVE BEHAVIORAL THERAPY (CBT)

SKILLS TRAINING TO MANAGE THOUGHTS & BEHAVIORS

DIALECTICAL BEHAVIOR THERAPY (DBT)

SKILLS TRAINING TO MANAGE EMOTIONS, THOUGHTS, & BEHAVIORS

PSYCHOEDUCATION

LEARNING ABOUT YOUR ILLNESS, & COMMUNICATION IN RELATIONSHIPS

INTERPERSONAL SOCIAL RHYTHM THERAPY (IPSRT)

FOCUSES ON MAINTAINING A STRUCTURED ROUTINE

SUPPORT GROUPS

ESPECIALLY USEFUL FOR MAINTAINING LONG-TERM STABILITY

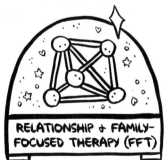

RELATIONSHIP & FAMILY-FOCUSED THERAPY (FFT)

GROUP THERAPY WITH GOALS SIMILAR TO PSYCHOEDUCATION

THIS, THAT

COMBINATIONS THEREOF, & ALTERNATIVE & EXPERIMENTAL THERAPIES

① PSYCHOTHERAPY, OR "TALK THERAPY"

FINDING & MAINTAINING STABILITY IS AN ENORMOUS UNDERTAKING THAT REALLY CALLS FOR A KNOWLEDGEABLE GUIDE THAT YOU TRUST.

THERE'S JUST SO MUCH TO UNDERSTAND & WORK THROUGH ABOUT THE ILLNESS & ABOUT OURSELVES.

ALSO, IF YOU FIND YOURSELF IN A CRISIS, YOU NEED SOMEONE WHO KNOWS YOU & YOUR PATTERNS.

TALK THERAPY USUALLY STARTS WITH ONE OR TWO SESSIONS A WEEK, THEN FEWER OVER TIME.

SOME PSYCHIATRISTS (LIKE MINE) DO TALK THERAPY, BUT IT'S USUALLY A PSYCHOLOGIST OR SOCIAL WORKER, & THEY WORK WITH A PSYCHIATRIST FOR PRESCRIBING MEDS.

I'VE HAD THE SAME PSYCHIATRIST FOR 20 YEARS (!!), & THE TIMING HAS VARIED FROM A COUPLE TIMES A WEEK TO ONCE EVERY 3 MONTHS.

TALK THERAPY IS INCORPORATED INTO MOST OTHER KINDS OF THERAPY, TOO.

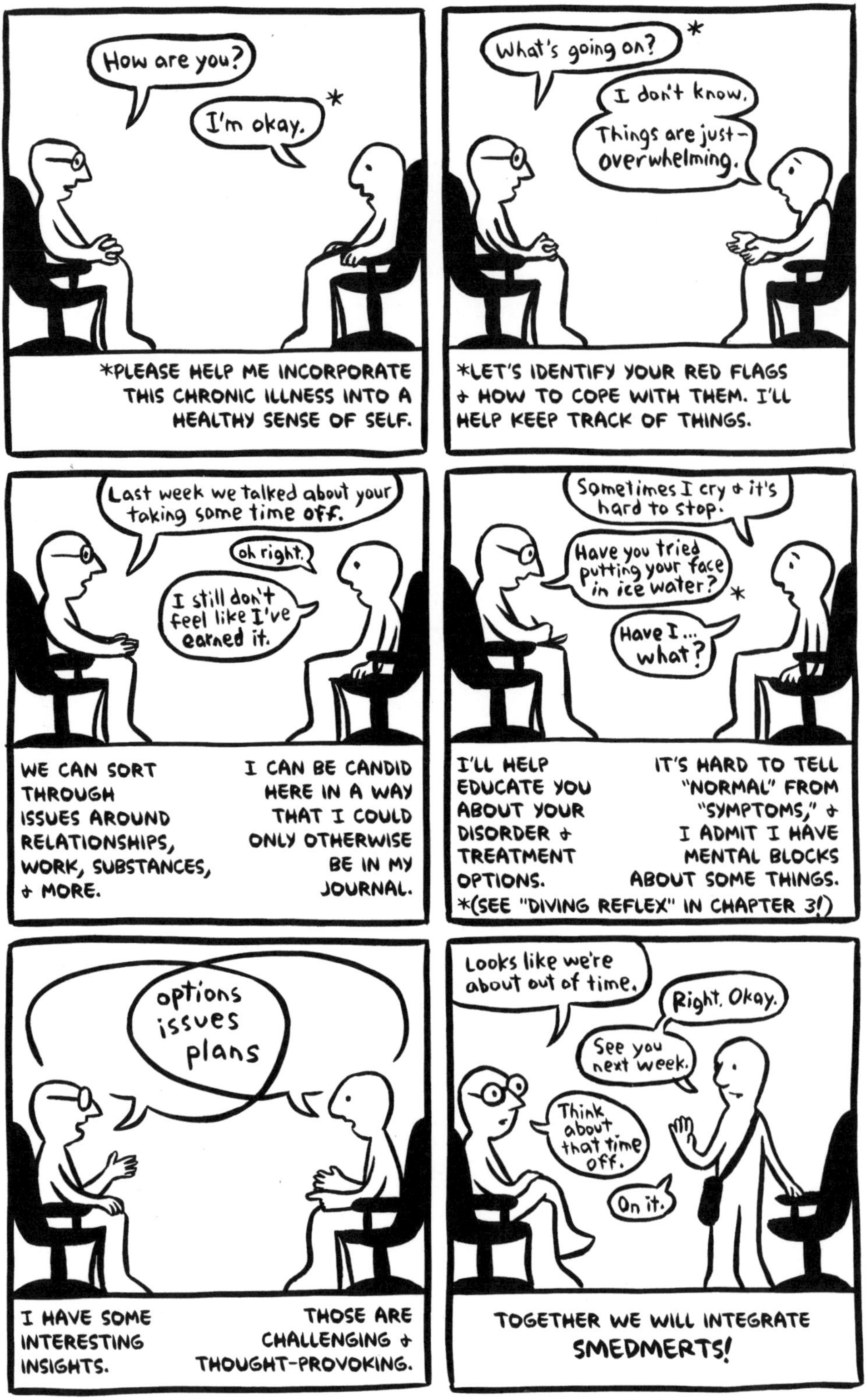
How are you?
I'm okay.*
*PLEASE HELP ME INCORPORATE THIS CHRONIC ILLNESS INTO A HEALTHY SENSE OF SELF.
What's going on?*
I don't know.
Things are just-overwhelming.
*LET'S IDENTIFY YOUR RED FLAGS & HOW TO COPE WITH THEM. I'LL HELP KEEP TRACK OF THINGS.
Last week we talked about your taking some time off.
oh right.
I still don't feel like I've earned it.
WE CAN SORT THROUGH ISSUES AROUND RELATIONSHIPS, WORK, SUBSTANCES, & MORE.
I CAN BE CANDID HERE IN A WAY THAT I COULD ONLY OTHERWISE BE IN MY JOURNAL.
Sometimes I cry & it's hard to stop.
Have you tried putting your face in ice water?*
Have I... what?
I'LL HELP EDUCATE YOU ABOUT YOUR DISORDER & TREATMENT OPTIONS.
IT'S HARD TO TELL "NORMAL" FROM "SYMPTOMS," & I ADMIT I HAVE MENTAL BLOCKS ABOUT SOME THINGS.
*(SEE "DIVING REFLEX" IN CHAPTER 3!)
options issues plans
I HAVE SOME INTERESTING INSIGHTS.
THOSE ARE CHALLENGING & THOUGHT-PROVOKING.
Looks like we're about out of time.
Right. Okay.
See you next week.
Think about that time off.
On it.
TOGETHER WE WILL INTEGRATE SMEDMERTS!

② MEDICATION

MEDICATION IS ONE OF THE MOST COMMON – & FOR MANY PEOPLE, ESSENTIAL – TREATMENTS FOR MOOD DISORDERS. IT MIGHT BE USED FOR A SHORT TIME AT THE BEGINNING OF THERAPY, &/OR FOR THE LONG TERM TO STAY STABLE & PREVENT FUTURE EPISODES, &/OR AS NEEDED FOR SLEEPING, SPECIFIC SITUATIONS, OR IN CRISIS.

MEDS ARE PRESCRIBED BY A MEDICAL DOCTOR, TYPICALLY A PSYCHIATRIST. SOMETIMES GENERAL PRACTITIONERS PRESCRIBE OR REFILL PSYCH MEDS, BUT OVERSIGHT & IMPORTANT TREATMENT DECISIONS NEED TO BE WITH A **THERAPIST**.

Rx — SOME CAUTIONS!

✔ MEDS ARE ARGUABLY OVERPRESCRIBED RIGHT NOW. BE SURE TO CONSIDER YOUR OPTIONS – DON'T MESS WITH YOUR NEURONS IF YOU DON'T HAVE TO!

✔ MOOD DISORDERS HAVE BIOLOGICAL AND PSYCHOLOGICAL AND SOCIAL ASPECTS, SO MEDS ALONE RARELY DO THE TRICK. (SO, LIKE, JUST SAY **NO** TO PSYCHOPHARMACOLOGICAL MONOTHERAPY...!)

✔ ANTIDEPRESSANTS CAN KICK IN A MANIC EPISODE FOR SOME PEOPLE WITH BIPOLAR.

✔ RESEARCH YOUR MEDS! SIDE EFFECTS FOR SHORT-TERM USE MAY BE DIFFERENT FROM LONG-TERM, IN PARTICULAR FOR SOME COMMONLY PRESCRIBED ATYPICAL ANTIPSYCHOTICS. MAKE SURE THE DOCTOR PRESCRIBING THEM STAYS ON TOP OF THE LAB WORK, TOO.

Refill —times: please specify a number between never & forever. ✔

③ COGNITIVE BEHAVIORAL THERAPY
...BETTER KNOWN AS CBT

CBT IS BASED ON THE IDEA THAT NEGATIVE MOODS & SELF-DEFEATING BEHAVIOR ARE CAUSED BY DISTORTED THOUGHTS & BELIEFS, & THAT TRAINING CAN HELP IDENTIFY & CORRECT THOSE PATTERNS.

CBT IS VERY STRUCTURED, & INVOLVES CHARTS, PERCENTAGE POINTS, SCALES, LISTS, WORKSHEETS... LOTS OF THAT, & TALK THERAPY.

HERE'S ONE CBT EXERCISE I PERSONALLY FOUND HELPFUL FOR THE SELF-BERATING THAT COMES WITH DEPRESSION.

"TALK BACK TO THAT INTERNAL CRITIC"

LIST NEGATIVE "AUTOMATIC THOUGHTS"

LIST "RATIONAL RESPONSES" TO THOSE THOUGHTS

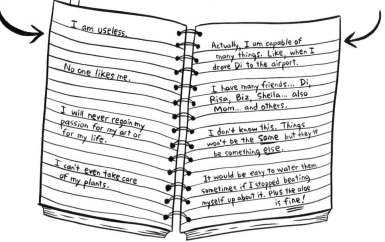

I am useless.

Actually, I am capable of many things. Like, when I drove Di to the airport.

No one likes me.

I have many friends... Di, Risa, Biz, Sheila... also Mom... and others.

I will never regain my passion for my art or for my life.

I don't know this. Things won't be the same but they'll be something else.

I can't even take care of my plants.

It would be easy to water them sometimes if I stopped beating myself up about it. Plus the aloe is fine!

THE NAME REFERS TO:

⭐ **COGNITIVE PSYCHOLOGY,** WHICH FOCUSES ON CONSCIOUS THOUGHT (E.G. REMEMBERING, BELIEVING, EXPECTING);

⭐ **BEHAVIORISM,** BASED ON THE THEORY THAT THOUGHTS, FEELINGS, & BEHAVIOR ARE MEASURABLE.

NOTE: CBT IS HELPFUL WITH DEPRESSION, MAINTENANCE, & DANGER SIGNS, BUT LIMITED HELP WITH FULL-ON MANIA.

④ DIALECTICAL BEHAVIOR THERAPY
...BETTER KNOWN AS DBT

DBT FOCUSES ON SKILLS TRAINING TO MANAGE THOUGHTS & EMOTIONS, TO BOTH ACCEPT THE SELF AND CREATE CHANGE. THE AIMS ARE TO BE IN THE PRESENT MOMENT, DEAL WITH OTHER PEOPLE, & TOLERATE BEING UPSET WITHOUT GETTING INTO A CRISIS.

LIKE CBT, DBT IS VERY STRUCTURED, WITH ONE-ON-ONE & GROUP MEETINGS, WORKSHEETS, & HOMEWORK, & A BIG FOCUS ON MINDFULNESS.

OBSERVING EMOTIONS

RELAPSE PREVENTION PLANNING

SELF-COMPASSION SKILLS

MINDFUL FOCUS PRACTICE

ONE VERY EFFECTIVE DBT DISTRESS TOLERANCE SKILL IS THE "DIVING REFLEX" – SEE CHAPTER 6!

A COOL THING: THE FOUNDER, DR. MARSHA LINEHAN, IS PUBLIC ABOUT HER OWN HISTORY OF BORDERLINE, SUICIDALITY, & HOSPITALIZATION.

THE NAME REFERS TO:

☆ **DIALECTICS,** THE PHILOSOPHY THAT TRUTH IS THE STRUGGLE & SYNTHESIS OF OPPOSITES, CREATING A DYNAMIC BALANCE (DR. LINEHAN WAS INSPIRED BY HER STUDY OF ZEN);

☆ **BEHAVIORISM,** AS IN CBT; ALSO THAT THOUGHTS, FEELINGS, & BEHAVIOR ARE BASED ON PAST EXPERIENCE (E.G., HOW TRAUMA IN THE PAST AFFECTS CERTAIN BEHAVIOR IN THE PRESENT).

NOTE: LIKE CBT, DBT IS EFFECTIVE FOR DEPRESSION, MAINTENANCE, & RECOGNIZING DANGER SIGNS, BUT LIMITED HELP WITH FULL-ON MANIA.

⑤ PSYCHOEDUCATION

LEARNING ABOUT YOUR DISORDER IS IMPORTANT FOR EVERYONE!

BEING KNOWLEDGEABLE ABOUT MENTAL HEALTH ISSUES CAN HELP YOU--

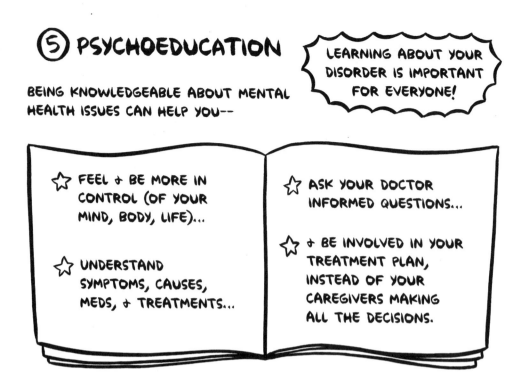

☆ FEEL & BE MORE IN CONTROL (OF YOUR MIND, BODY, LIFE)...

☆ UNDERSTAND SYMPTOMS, CAUSES, MEDS, & TREATMENTS...

☆ ASK YOUR DOCTOR INFORMED QUESTIONS...

☆ & BE INVOLVED IN YOUR TREATMENT PLAN, INSTEAD OF YOUR CAREGIVERS MAKING ALL THE DECISIONS.

IN PRACTICE, PSYCHOEDUCATION INVOLVES TALK THERAPY ONE-ON-ONE, IN A GROUP WITH A DISCUSSION LEADER, & IN GROUP FAMILY SESSIONS WITH A THERAPIST; & ANY INFORMATION-GATHERING FROM REFERENCE SOURCES OR PEOPLE.

IMPORTANT: USE SOURCES YOU TRUST.
SOME GOOD ONES--

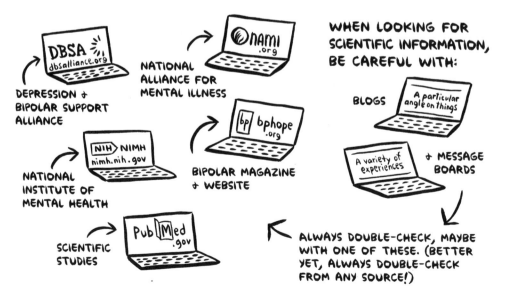

DBSA dbsalliance.org

DEPRESSION & BIPOLAR SUPPORT ALLIANCE

nami.org

NATIONAL ALLIANCE FOR MENTAL ILLNESS

NIH NIMH nimh.nih.gov

NATIONAL INSTITUTE OF MENTAL HEALTH

bp bphope.org

BIPOLAR MAGAZINE & WEBSITE

PubMed.gov

SCIENTIFIC STUDIES

WHEN LOOKING FOR SCIENTIFIC INFORMATION, BE CAREFUL WITH:

BLOGS — A particular angle on things

A variety of experiences

& MESSAGE BOARDS

ALWAYS DOUBLE-CHECK, MAYBE WITH ONE OF THESE. (BETTER YET, ALWAYS DOUBLE-CHECK FROM ANY SOURCE!)

⑥ INTERPERSONAL & SOCIAL RHYTHM THERAPY

IPSRT FOCUSES ON KEEPING A STRUCTURED ROUTINE AROUND CIRCADIAN RHYTHMS (OUR BODY CLOCK) WITH A PARTICULAR FOCUS ON SLEEP PATTERNS.

THE NAME REFERS TO:

INTERPERSONAL PSYCHOTHERAPY (IPT),
FOCUSING ON THE IMPORTANCE OF RELATIONSHIPS & HOW MOODS & LIFE EVENTS AFFECT EACH OTHER;

SOCIAL RHYTHM THERAPY (SRT),
FOCUSING ON MAINTAINING A DAILY ROUTINE.

IN PRACTICE, IPSRT INVOLVES INDIVIDUAL APPOINTMENTS WITH A PSYCHOTHERAPIST, USING CBT-STYLE EXERCISES FOR IDENTIFYING & TRACKING PATTERNS, & PLANNING FOR FUTURE DISRUPTIONS (E.G. JOB CHANGES OR JET LAG FROM TRAVEL).

A SAMPLE IPSRT EXERCISE IS IN CHAPTER 6, IN THE SECTION ON CHARTING.

⑦ SUPPORT GROUPS

SUPPORT GROUPS ARE DIFFERENT FROM GROUP THERAPY IN THAT SUPPORT GROUPS ARE GENERALLY LED BY A PEER OR TRAINED VOLUNTEER & ARE FREE, AND GROUP THERAPY IS RUN BY A THERAPIST & COSTS MONEY.

ONLINE MESSAGE BOARDS & CHAT ROOMS ARE MORE CONVENIENT, BUT SITTING IN A ROOM OF OTHER LIVING, BREATHING BIPOLAR PEOPLE WAS A PRETTY AMAZING EXPERIENCE FOR ME.

TO FIND A SUPPORT GROUP, TRY NAMI.ORG OR DBSA.ORG - THEY LIST THE CLOSEST GROUP BY ZIP CODE.

GROUPS SHARE COMPANY, COPING TECHNIQUES, & IDEAS. SUPPORT FROM PEOPLE WITH THE SAME DISORDER HELPS WITH LONG-TERM MAINTENANCE & DECREASES RATES OF HOSPITALIZATION. (STUDIES SHOW!)

⑧ FAMILY FOCUSED THERAPY

IN FFT, PATIENT & PARTNER OR FAMILY MEMBERS GO THROUGH TALK THERAPY TOGETHER TO LEARN ABOUT THE DISORDER & WORK ON COMMUNICATION & PROBLEM-SOLVING SKILLS.

IN PRACTICE, IT'S USUALLY 21 SESSIONS OVER NINE MONTHS – WEEKLY, BIWEEKLY, THEN MONTHLY.

FFT DOESN'T PRESUME THAT THE FAMILY IS DYSFUNCTIONAL, JUST THAT FAMILY DYNAMICS ARE IMPORTANT, & THAT A COLLABORATIVE APPROACH PLAYS AN IMPORTANT ROLE IN A PATIENT'S STABILITY.

⑨ OTHER THERAPIES

⭐ **ELECTROCONVULSIVE THERAPY** (ECT), YES, IS STILL AROUND: ELECTRIC CURRENTS ARE PASSED THROUGH THE BRAIN, CAUSING A BRIEF SEIZURE.

DESPITE SOUNDING REALLY SCARY & SOME SERIOUS SIDE EFFECTS (MEMORY LOSS, IN PARTICULAR), ECT IS CONSIDERED VERY EFFECTIVE FOR SEVERE DEPRESSION, ESPECIALLY WHEN MEDICATION HASN'T WORKED.

CARRIE FISHER WROTE APPRECIATIVELY ABOUT HER ECT TREATMENTS IN HER MEMOIR, SHOCKAHOLIC:

My brain had felt as though it was set in cement — the ECT blasted my Hoover Dam head wide open, moving the immovable.

Over time, this fucking thing punched the dark lights out of my depression.

True!

⭐ **DEEP BRAIN STIMULATION** (DBS) INVOLVES ELECTRODES IMPLANTED IN CERTAIN AREAS OF THE BRAIN, & AN ELECTRIC CURRENT IS USED TO REGULATE BRAIN ACTIVITY IN THOSE AREAS.

⭐ **ART THERAPY, MUSIC THERAPY, & ACUPUNCTURE** CAN ALSO HELP, & CERTAINLY SOME OTHER STUFF IS WORTH TRYING, & A LOT OF OTHER STUFF IS HOOEY.

⭐ **NEW & EXPERIMENTAL TREATMENTS & MEDICATIONS** ARE CONSTANTLY BEING INTRODUCED. PERSONALLY, I TEND TO BE WARY — I THINK LONG-TERM STUDIES ARE IMPORTANT. NO ONE REALLY KNOWS HOW THE BRAIN WORKS!

This expensive new drug that isn't covered by your insurance may help for a while according to this recent study on mice.

Watch out for suicidal thoughts!

Here's a sample!

We developed it by accident when we were testing ingredients in floor wax!

AND OF COURSE,

SMEDMERTS

NO MATTER WHAT OTHER
THERAPIES YOU'RE FOLLOWING.

Sleep

Meds

Eat

Doctor

Mindfulness

Exercise

Routine

Tools

Support system

SOMETIMES THINGS CAN GET **EXTRA OFF-BALANCE** - FROM STRESS, INEFFECTIVE TREATMENT, OR JUST BECAUSE WONKY BRAIN. GETTING DANGEROUSLY MANIC OR SUICIDAL MEANS MORE ACUTE TREATMENT.

HOSPITALIZATION IS,
BY ALMOST ALL ACCOUNTS,

A HUGE **DRAG** WITH MANY NON-THERAPEUTIC ASPECTS

AND

AN ESSENTIAL PLACE FOR FEELING & BEING **SAFE** IN A CRISIS, & TO **STABILIZE** WITH SLEEP, STRUCTURE, MEDS, & A BREAK FROM THE CRISIS-INDUCING CONTEXT.

IF YOU WANT TO BE PREPARED, YOU COULD RESEARCH YOUR PSYCH HOSPITAL OPTIONS IN ADVANCE.

DO THEY TAKE YOUR INSURANCE?

WHAT DO YOU THINK OF THE FACILITIES?

WHAT TREATMENT OPTIONS DO THEY OFFER?

ARE THERE ART PROGRAMS? EXERCISE OPTIONS?

WHAT ARE THE OUTDOOR AREAS LIKE?

WHAT'S NEARBY?

...WHAT'S IMPORTANT TO YOU?

?

(MORE ON HOSPITALIZATION IN CHAPTER 6.)

TREATMENT IS WHOA EXPENSIVE. WHAT TO DO?!
FINANCING YOUR MENTAL HEALTH

IT IS A SUCKY, SUCKY, SUCKY REALITY THAT IF YOU DON'T ALREADY HAVE CONSIDERABLE FINANCIAL RESOURCES, YOU WILL NEED TO BE (EVEN MORE) DILIGENT & CREATIVE.*

IF THE IDEA OF SEARCHING FOR SERVICES & MAKING PHONE CALLS SOUNDS IMPOSSIBLY EXHAUSTING, THIS WOULD BE A GOOD TIME TO TURN TO YOUR SUPPORT SYSTEM FOR HELP.

HERE ARE SOME IDEAS & RESOURCES...

 GET HELP BEFORE YOU'RE IN CRISIS. WATCH FOR RED FLAGS - MAYBE AN APPOINTMENT TO TALK OR ADJUST MEDS COULD AVERT AN EXPENSIVE ORDEAL.

 HAVE HEALTH INSURANCE. RESEARCH TO SEE IF YOU CAN GET FEDERAL OR STATE ASSISTANCE.

 MAKE SURE YOU KNOW WHAT YOUR INSURANCE DOES & DOESN'T COVER. REVIEW YOUR PLAN, OR CALL & ASK.

 PRIMARY CARE PHYSICIANS IN YOUR INSURANCE NETWORK MAY HELP WITH MED REFILLS.

TALK TO YOUR HEALTH CARE PROVIDER(S) & SEE IF YOU CAN WORK OUT LOWER FEES OR A PAYMENT PLAN, OR FIND A PROVIDER THAT CHARGES ON A SLIDING SCALE.

ASK YOUR DOCTOR TO CONTACT YOUR INSURANCE COMPANY TO SEE IF THEY WILL ALLOW MORE TREATMENT FOR YOU.

*DEAR READER, IT IS WINTER 2017. PERHAPS FUTURE HEALTH CARE IS FABULOUS!

☆ SCHEDULE THERAPY APPOINTMENTS WITH A LITTLE MORE TIME IN BETWEEN, & ASK YOUR DOCTOR ABOUT PHONE CHECK-INS.

☆ COMMUNITY MENTAL HEALTH CENTERS MAY OFFER INEXPENSIVE OR FREE INDIVIDUAL OR GROUP COUNSELING.

☆ CONTACT THE PHARMACEUTICAL COMPANY THAT MAKES YOUR MEDICATION & SEE IF YOU'RE ELIGIBLE FOR A FINANCIAL ASSISTANCE PROGRAM – THERE ARE SOMETIMES FORMS ONLINE – OR ASK YOUR DOCTOR TO CONTACT THEM.

☆ SAVE YOUR MONEY IN A FSA (FLEXIBLE SPENDING ACCOUNT), AN ACCOUNT FOR HEALTH CARE SERVICES THAT YOU DON'T HAVE TO PAY TAX ON.

☆ SUPPORT GROUPS ARE GENERALLY FREE.

☆ CHECK OUT DBT & CBT BOOKS & WORKBOOKS IN YOUR BOOKSTORE OR FROM YOUR PUBLIC LIBRARY.

☆ NAMI HAS MANY LINKS & A HELPLINE FOR INFORMATION, RESOURCES, & SERVICES IN YOUR AREA. (NAMI.ORG)

MERIT BADGES FOR
THERAPY
STRATEGIZING, HANDLING, HEALING

MIND

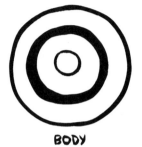

BODY

ENVIRONMENT

RESEARCH

ASK FOR HELP

EFFECTIVE
THERAPY(IES)

EFFECTIVE
THERAPIST(S)

PLANS FOR
HOSPITALIZATION
IF/WHEN
NECESSARY

FINANCE
EVERYTHING

CHAPTER 3
COPING TOOLS

MAINTAINING STABLILITY IS HARD. MEET THIS CHALLENGE TO EVEN OUT YOUR MOODS WITH AS MANY EMOTIONAL & LOGISTICAL TOOLS AS POSSIBLE, & THE KNOWLEDGE THAT YOU CAN FIND OR CREATE MORE, AS YOU NEED THEM.

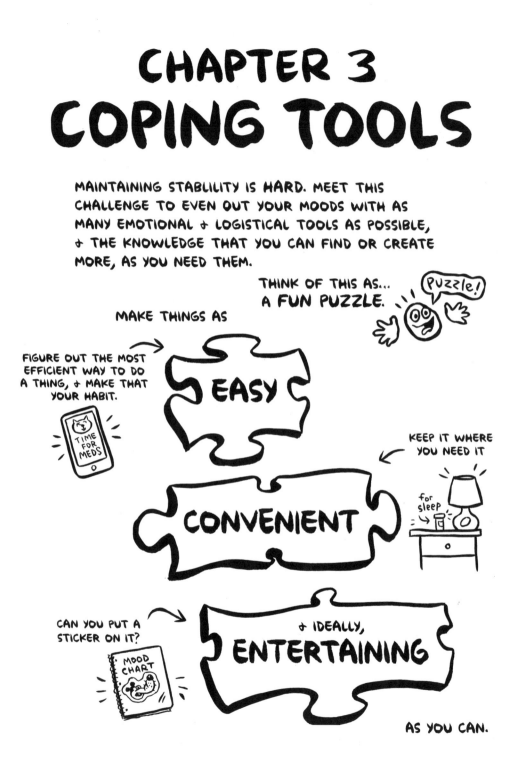

THINK OF THIS AS... A FUN PUZZLE.

PUZZLE!

MAKE THINGS AS

FIGURE OUT THE MOST EFFICIENT WAY TO DO A THING, & MAKE THAT YOUR HABIT.

TIME FOR MEDS

EASY

KEEP IT WHERE YOU NEED IT

for sleep

CONVENIENT

CAN YOU PUT A STICKER ON IT?

MOOD CHART

& IDEALLY, ENTERTAINING

AS YOU CAN.

YOU MIGHT THINK OF THESE TOOLS AS A RANGE OF:

EXTERNALIZING
& MORE ACTIVE THINGS..

INTERNALIZING
& MORE PASSIVE THINGS...

& PLENTY OF SOOTHING
& SELF-COMPASSIONATE THINGS.

MOST OF THESE TOOLS AREN'T SPECIFIC TO A PARTICULAR MOOD STATE. THEY'RE ABOUT **CALMING & CENTERING** – TECHNIQUES YOU CAN WORK INTO YOUR LIFE TO HELP MAINTAIN BALANCE, & WAYS TO CALIBRATE WHEN YOU'RE FEELING OUT OF WHACK.

CREATIVE THINGS ARE GREAT IN A ZILLION WAYS. YOU CAN GET YOUR EMOTIONS OUT, PROCESS, BE CONCRETE, BE ABSTRACT, FOCUS, LET GO. EVEN IF "CREATIVITY" IS NOT GENERALLY YOUR "THING," PUTTING STUFF TOGETHER CAN BE VERY SATISFYING.

● JOURNAL.

YOU CAN **REALLY** BE CANDID & LET GO IN A JOURNAL.

IT'S ALSO AN EXCELLENT WAY TO TRACK YOUR MOODS.

● DRAW.

EVEN JUST SITTING & DRAWING LINES & SHAPES, OR USING COLORS, CAN BE COMFORTING. DRAWING A THING CAN TAKE THE FOCUS OUTSIDE OF YOURSELF, & MAY BE EASIER THAN TRYING TO FIND THE RIGHT WORDS.

I DRAW A LOT OF SELF-PORTRAITS IN MY SKETCHBOOKS & JOURNALS.

I can't stop crying.

OKAY,
Got this.

SPACE CADETTE

SEE THIS DRAWING *IN ACTION* IN CHAPTER 7!

DON'T KNOW WHAT TO DRAW? HAVEN'T DRAWN SINCE YOU WERE A KID?

● JUST MAKE MARKS ON PAPER.

SPIRALS

MANDALAS

DRAW CONCENTRIC CIRCLES & STRAIGHT LINES THAT RADIATE FROM THE CENTER, THEN FILL IN PATTERNS. (MORE INFO AND TEMPLATES ONLINE!)

KIDS' OR ADULT COLORING BOOKS

TRACE SOMETHING.

MANDALA -O- RAMA TEMPLATES

Color Wix' Pokémon

COLOR ME Kama Sutra

WHAT'S YOUR THING?

● DO THAT THING.

OR JUST GO THROUGH THE MOTIONS, IF IT'S NOT COMING EASILY.

PLAY MUSIC.

MAKE COMICS.

MEANWHILE...

WRITE STORIES.
WRITE POEMS.

KNIT.
EMBROIDER.
MAKE A
HOOK RUG.

IF CREATIVE OUTPUT REALLY ISN'T GOING TO DO IT...

CREATIVE INPUT MIGHT BE THE THING.

THERE'S PLENTY TO READ, WATCH, & LISTEN TO BY ARTISTS THAT WRESTLE WITH SIMILAR ISSUES.

+ Episode IV: ♪
HOSPITAL SUITE
HOSPITAL

The Moody Shoes

!#@! IN the DARK

Light At The Tunnel's End

(LOTS OF ACTUAL EXAMPLES ARE IN CHAPTER 7.)

ALLOW YOURSELF THINGS THAT COMFORT YOU

EVEN IF THEY SEEM SILLY OR INDULGENT.

STUFFED ANIMAL

MATINEE

MIDDAY THEATRE
ADMIT ONE | FUNNY CUTE ANIMATED TREAT
IN HD 3D $ CHEAP

BEESWAX CANDLES

ONCE WHEN I WAS REALLY LOW, I WAS CONFLICTED ABOUT THIS TOOL. I REALLY WANTED A STUFFED ANIMAL, BUT I WAS ALREADY STRUGGLING WITH FEELING LIKE A BIG BABY.

THEN I HAD AN IDEA FOR A STAND-IN:

BIG SOFT FUZZY PILLOW

THIS WORKED GREAT!

BE KIND TO YOURSELF.

SELF-COMPASSION CAN BE DIFFICULT FOR ANYONE, BUT IT MIGHT NOT EVEN OCCUR TO YOU IF YOU'RE DEPRESSED.

WOW, COULD I BERATE MYSELF WHEN I WAS DOWN.

← my own foot

IF YOUR INNER VOICE IS GETTING REALLY HARSH...

snap!

Gah! I'm such an idiot!!

..THINK OF IT AS A FURIOUS ADULT BERATING AN INCONSOLABLE CHILD. UGH. NEITHER HAS REASON TO CALM DOWN, BOTH FEEL WORSE & WORSE. IT'S A MISERABLE PLACE TO GET STUCK.

I broke it I'm sorry aaaaaa aaaaaa!!

little you →

Gah! You're such an idiot!!

←bully you

SO... TAKE A STEP BACK. BREATHE.

(THIS IS NOT EASY! MANY TOOLS FOR CALMING YOURSELF ARE IN THIS & FOLLOWING CHAPTERS.)

inhale   exhale

breath   breath

THINK OF SOMEONE YOU TRULY, INTUITIVELY CARE ABOUT.

NIECE   BEST FRIEND   ANYONE YOU ♡

CONSIDER HOW YOU MIGHT TREAT THEM IN THIS SITUATION – ESPECIALLY, HOW YOU MIGHT TREAT THEM IF THEY WERE BERATING THEMSELVES.

Aaaaa!! I broke it, I'm sorry! I'm such an idiot!!

Oh no! Well, that sucks but shh-- it's okay!

NOW MENTALLY REPLACE THEM WITH YOU...

I broke it I'm sorry!! Sob!!

Oh no! Well, that sucks but shh-- it's okay!

.. ....

I'm really depressed.

I know... it's hard. It's okay.

... & TREAT YOURSELF LIKE THAT.

THIS TRICK COULD SOMETIMES HELP ME RECOGNIZE THE FUTILITY OF THAT STUCK, BERATING PLACE, & GET BEYOND IT.

Oh no! This sucks. Shh-- it's okay.

I'm really depressed. It's hard. I know. It's okay.

FOCUS ON YOUR PHYSICAL BODY

IF THE FLU MAKES YOU FEEL DOWN, + A MASSAGE MAKES YOU FEEL CALM, THEN YOU KNOW WHAT AFFECTS YOUR BODY ALSO AFFECTS YOUR MOODS.

BODY SCAN

CONCENTRATE ON DIFFERENT PARTS OF YOUR BODY, ONE BY ONE. ARE YOU TENSE ANYWHERE IN PARTICULAR?

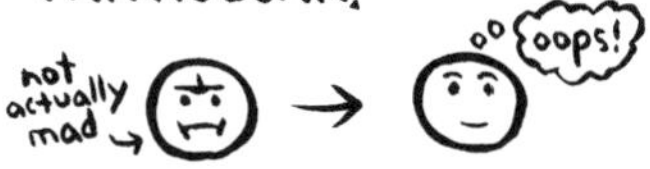
not actually mad
oops!

I TEND TO SCRUNCH MY FACE.

YOU MIGHT TRY TENSING YOUR ENTIRE BODY...

+ THEN RELAXING EVERYTHING.

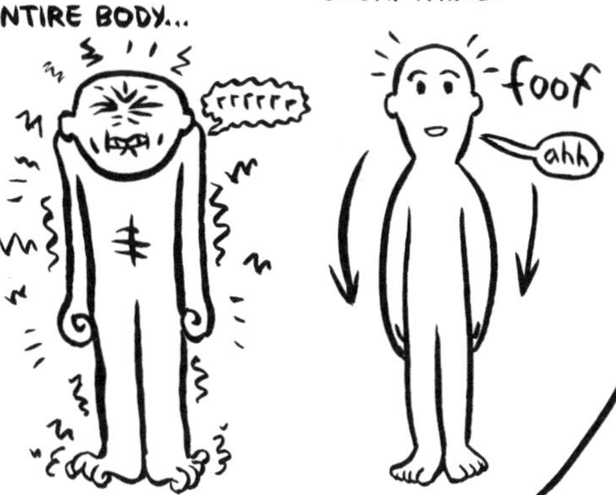
rrrrrr
foof
ahh

TAKE A SHOWER OR BATH

EVEN A QUICK ONE CAN RESET YOUR MOOD.

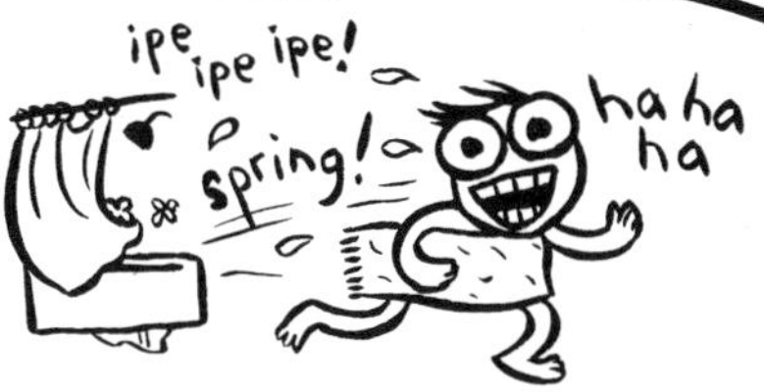
ipe ipe ipe!
spring!
ha ha ha

INVIGORATING SHOWER OPTION THAT I PERSONALLY LOVE: END WITH FREEZING COLD! **REBOOT!!!**

POSTURE

STANDING OR SITTING DIFFERENTLY CAN CHANGE YOUR MOOD A LOT.

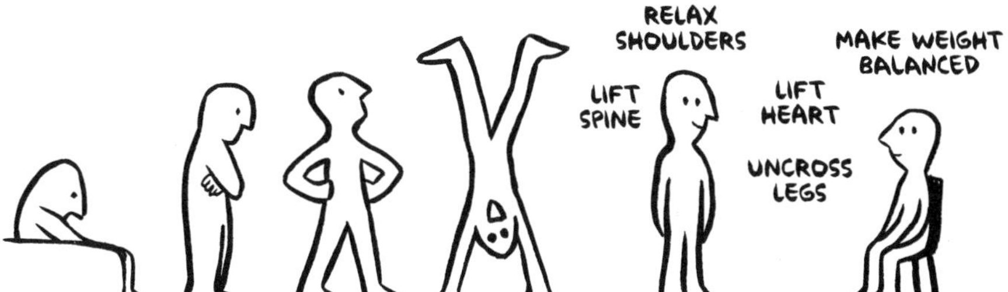
RELAX SHOULDERS
LIFT SPINE
LIFT HEART
UNCROSS LEGS
MAKE WEIGHT BALANCED

• SOME MOVING AROUND
(ASIDE FROM YOUR REGULAR EXERCISE ROUTINE)

DOING A BIT OF LOW-KEY EXERCISE — EVEN JUST A TINY BIT — CAN TURN AROUND AN EMOTION THAT IS NOT SERVING YOU.

EVEN BETTER IF YOU CAN GET OUTSIDE.

⭐ BREATHING

SLOWING & PAYING ATTENTION TO YOUR BREATH WILL CALM YOU, EVEN IF YOUR MIND IS ALL OVER THE PLACE.
BREATHING IS A POWERFUL & CONVENIENT TOOL – IN A CRISIS, ON THE COUCH, WHILE RUSHING SOMEWHERE, OR WHENEVER.

⬤ BREATHE FULLY.

INHALE THROUGH YOUR NOSE, & EXHALE THROUGH YOUR NOSE OR SLIGHTLY PURSED LIPS.

PUT A HAND ON YOUR CHEST & A HAND ON YOUR BELLY.	INHALE INTO YOUR CHEST, UNDER YOUR CHEST HAND...	...& DOWN INTO YOUR BELLY, UNDER YOUR BELLY HAND.
EXHALE FROM YOUR BELLY, ENGAGING YOUR ABS LITTLE...	...THEN FROM YOUR CHEST.	INHALE CHEST... BELLY... EXHALE BELLY... CHEST. INHALE CHEST... BELLY... EXHALE BELLY... CHEST.

OUR BREATH TENDS TO GET VERY SHALLOW WHEN WE GET STRESSED OUT, & WE BREATHE JUST FROM OUR CHESTS. I CATCH MYSELF DOING THAT A FAIR BIT.

Oh jeez- I don't think I'm breathing at all!

● EXHALING SLOWLY

CAN BE DIFFICULT WHEN YOU'RE UPSET.

ONE WAY TO SLOW YOUR EXHALES IS BY NARROWING YOUR THROAT. THAT WAY YOU CAN ALSO **HEAR** YOUR EXHALES, WHICH HELPS KEEP YOUR BREATHING SLOW & EVEN.

IT'S SIMILAR TO HOW NARROWING YOUR LIPS CONTROLS THE SPEED & FLOW OF WHAT YOU'RE DRINKING.

NARROW OPENING OF LIPS = SLOW

WIDE OPENING OF LIPS = FAST

IN YOGA, THIS TECHNIQUE IS CALLED "UJJAYI" (RHYMES WITH "OOH, CHAI")  OR "VICTORIOUS BREATH." HERE'S HOW MY YOGA TEACHER EXPLAINS IT:

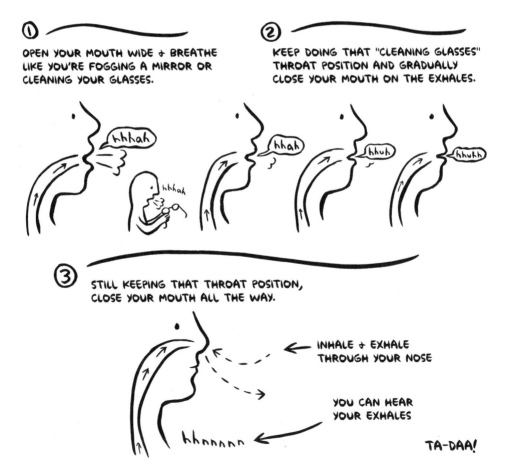

① OPEN YOUR MOUTH WIDE & BREATHE LIKE YOU'RE FOGGING A MIRROR OR CLEANING YOUR GLASSES.

② KEEP DOING THAT "CLEANING GLASSES" THROAT POSITION AND GRADUALLY CLOSE YOUR MOUTH ON THE EXHALES.

③ STILL KEEPING THAT THROAT POSITION, CLOSE YOUR MOUTH ALL THE WAY.

INHALE & EXHALE THROUGH YOUR NOSE

YOU CAN HEAR YOUR EXHALES

TA-DAA!

TAKE **FIVE DEEP BREATHS** ANYTIME.

MY BAROMETER FOR HOW FRAZZLED I AM IS IF I FEEL LIKE I ONLY HAVE TIME FOR THREE.

IF YOU'RE PANICKING, YOUR BREATH IS PROBABLY UNEVEN OR RAPID. YOU CAN EVEN IT OUT BY COUNTING THE LENGTHS OF YOUR INHALES & EXHALES.

SYMMETRICAL BREATHING

BREATHE IN FOR 2 COUNTS...

& OUT FOR 2 COUNTS...

IN FOR 2 COUNTS...

& OUT FOR 2 COUNTS...

KEEP REPEATING.

● ASYMMETRICAL BREATHING

BREATHE IN FOR 2 COUNTS...

& OUT FOR 4 COUNTS...

IN FOR 2 COUNTS...

& OUT FOR 4 COUNTS...

KEEP REPEATING.

● ALTERNATE NOSTRIL BREATHING
CALMING & BALANCING. A PERSONAL FAVORITE.

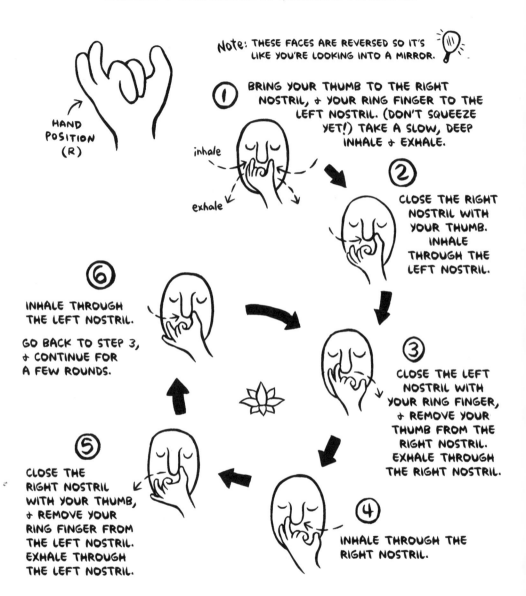

HAND POSITION (R)

Note: THESE FACES ARE REVERSED SO IT'S LIKE YOU'RE LOOKING INTO A MIRROR.

① BRING YOUR THUMB TO THE RIGHT NOSTRIL, & YOUR RING FINGER TO THE LEFT NOSTRIL. (DON'T SQUEEZE YET!) TAKE A SLOW, DEEP INHALE & EXHALE.

inhale

exhale

② CLOSE THE RIGHT NOSTRIL WITH YOUR THUMB. INHALE THROUGH THE LEFT NOSTRIL.

⑥ INHALE THROUGH THE LEFT NOSTRIL.

GO BACK TO STEP 3, & CONTINUE FOR A FEW ROUNDS.

③ CLOSE THE LEFT NOSTRIL WITH YOUR RING FINGER, & REMOVE YOUR THUMB FROM THE RIGHT NOSTRIL. EXHALE THROUGH THE RIGHT NOSTRIL.

⑤ CLOSE THE RIGHT NOSTRIL WITH YOUR THUMB, & REMOVE YOUR RING FINGER FROM THE LEFT NOSTRIL. EXHALE THROUGH THE LEFT NOSTRIL.

④ INHALE THROUGH THE RIGHT NOSTRIL.

ANOTHER OPTION FOR HAND POSITION: PUT YOUR INDEX & MIDDLE FINGERS TO THE CENTER OF YOUR FOREHEAD (YOUR "THIRD EYE," IF YOU WILL).

THIS IS WHAT I USUALLY USE - I LIKE THE THIRD EYE THING & IT HELPS KEEP MY FOREHEAD RELAXED.

A LOVELY WAY TO COUNT 12 BREATHS

PUT YOUR THUMB TO YOUR FINGER PARTS ("PHALANGES") IN THIS ORDER – NOTE THAT IT IS A SPIRAL.

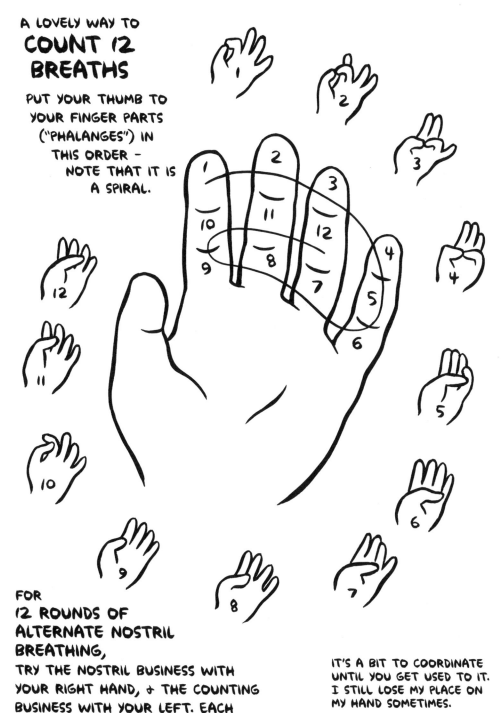

FOR
12 ROUNDS OF ALTERNATE NOSTRIL BREATHING,

TRY THE NOSTRIL BUSINESS WITH YOUR RIGHT HAND, & THE COUNTING BUSINESS WITH YOUR LEFT. EACH ROUND FINISHES WHEN YOU EXHALE THROUGH YOUR LEFT NOSTRIL.

(12 ROUNDS TAKES ABOUT 5 MINUTES.)

IT'S A BIT TO COORDINATE UNTIL YOU GET USED TO IT. I STILL LOSE MY PLACE ON MY HAND SOMETIMES.

LAND OF THUMB & FINGERS

HAVE A REGULAR

MEDITATION *MINDFULNESS
PRACTICE

IT'S REALLY HARD TO CALM DOWN & BE "IN THE MOMENT" WHEN YOU'RE STRESSED OUT, SO IT'S USEFUL TO PRACTICE REGULARLY WHILE YOU'RE **NOT** STRESSED.

THERE'S PRACTICING IN STILLNESS, & PRACTICING IN THE WORLD.

FOR PRACTICING IN STILLNESS,

● PICK A REGULAR TIME

START WITH A HANDLEABLE DURATION & TIME OF DAY, SOMETHING YOU CAN STICK WITH.

FOR 15 MINS IN THE MORNING? FOR 20 MINS BEFORE BED? 5? 30?

IDEALLY, YOUR PRACTICE IS PART OF YOUR DAILY RHYTHM. BUT YOU KNOW – WHATEVER YOU CAN DO IS GREAT.

● FIND A COMFORTABLE POSITION
YOU DON'T NECESSARILY HAVE TO SIT LIKE A YOGI.

SIT AGAINST A WALL

PROPS (I FINALLY REALIZED I NEED LOTS OF THESE!)

me: 1 couch 1 rolled yoga mat 3 pillows

A SEAT

LYING DOWN (TRY NOT TO FALL ASLEEP THOUGH!)

● TRY DIFFERENT WAYS TO FOCUS

EYES OPEN   OR CLOSED

SET A TIMER FOR EVERY 5 MINS AS A REMINDER TO QUIET YOUR MIND

A GUIDED MEDITATION (SMART PHONE APP, WEBSITE, SOMETHING FROM YOUR LIBRARY)

blah blah   ting!

"WHITE NOISE" IN HEADPHONES FOR A PORTABLE CALM SPACE

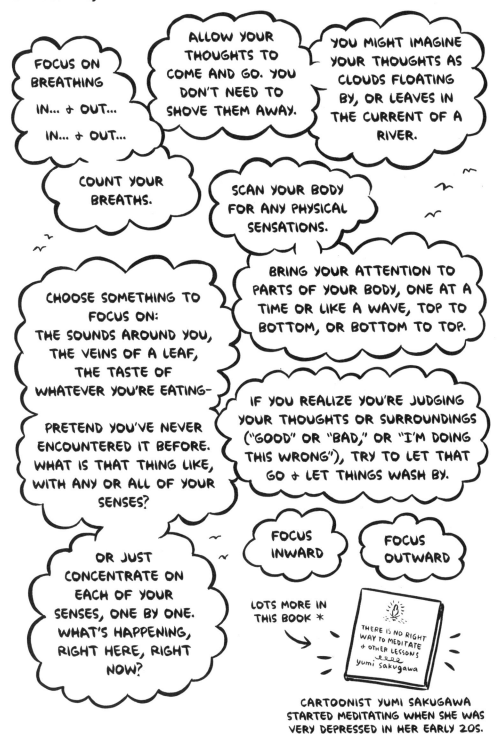

FOCUS ON BREATHING

IN... & OUT...

IN... & OUT...

ALLOW YOUR THOUGHTS TO COME AND GO. YOU DON'T NEED TO SHOVE THEM AWAY.

YOU MIGHT IMAGINE YOUR THOUGHTS AS CLOUDS FLOATING BY, OR LEAVES IN THE CURRENT OF A RIVER.

COUNT YOUR BREATHS.

SCAN YOUR BODY FOR ANY PHYSICAL SENSATIONS.

CHOOSE SOMETHING TO FOCUS ON:
THE SOUNDS AROUND YOU,
THE VEINS OF A LEAF,
THE TASTE OF WHATEVER YOU'RE EATING–

PRETEND YOU'VE NEVER ENCOUNTERED IT BEFORE. WHAT IS THAT THING LIKE, WITH ANY OR ALL OF YOUR SENSES?

BRING YOUR ATTENTION TO PARTS OF YOUR BODY, ONE AT A TIME OR LIKE A WAVE, TOP TO BOTTOM, OR BOTTOM TO TOP.

IF YOU REALIZE YOU'RE JUDGING YOUR THOUGHTS OR SURROUNDINGS ("GOOD" OR "BAD," OR "I'M DOING THIS WRONG"), TRY TO LET THAT GO & LET THINGS WASH BY.

FOCUS INWARD

FOCUS OUTWARD

OR JUST CONCENTRATE ON EACH OF YOUR SENSES, ONE BY ONE. WHAT'S HAPPENING, RIGHT HERE, RIGHT NOW?

LOTS MORE IN THIS BOOK *

THERE IS NO RIGHT WAY TO MEDITATE & OTHER LESSONS
yumi sakugawa

CARTOONIST YUMI SAKUGAWA STARTED MEDITATING WHEN SHE WAS VERY DEPRESSED IN HER EARLY 20S.

* THERE IS NO RIGHT WAY TO MEDITATE, BY YUMI SAKUGAWA (ADAMS MEDIA, 2015)

⭐ AN OCCASIONAL BOOST,
ESPECIALLY WHEN STRESSING--
10 MINUTES... 5 MINUTES... ONE MINUTE, EVEN.

IN PUBLIC--

I SAW A MOTORCYCLE DUDE
MEDITATING ON THE FERRY ONCE.

A PRIVATE MOMENT IN
A PUBLIC AREA --

DOING LAUNDRY --

WAITING IN LINE.

SOMEPLACE MILDLY IRRITATING IS ACTUALLY
A GOOD PLACE TO PRACTICE QUIETING
YOUR BRAIN.

IT TOOK YEARS OF ABANDONED ATTEMPTS BEFORE I FIGURED OUT A
DAILY ROUTINE I COULD STICK WITH--

15 MINS YOGA
& 15 MINS
MEDITATION EVERY
MORNING, BEFORE
GETTING INVOLVED
IN THE DAY.

IF I REALLY DON'T
HAVE TIME, OR IF
I'M TRAVELING, I
MIGHT DO 5 MINS
AND 5 MINS, OR
12 BREATHS & 12
BREATHS.

THAT PRACTICE OF "BEING IN THE MOMENT" HAS BECOME ONE OF MY
MOST IMPORTANT TOOLS FOR MY MOOD, STRESS LEVEL, & SLEEP. HIGHLY
RECOMMENDED. FIVE STARS!

I'M NOT SURE IF I WAS "BEING IN THE MOMENT," EXACTLY... BUT I WOULD ARGUE THAT IT WAS GOOD PRACTICE!

SIDE-STEPPING WALKING MEDITATION

- OR -

ALIENS IN THE ARBORETUM

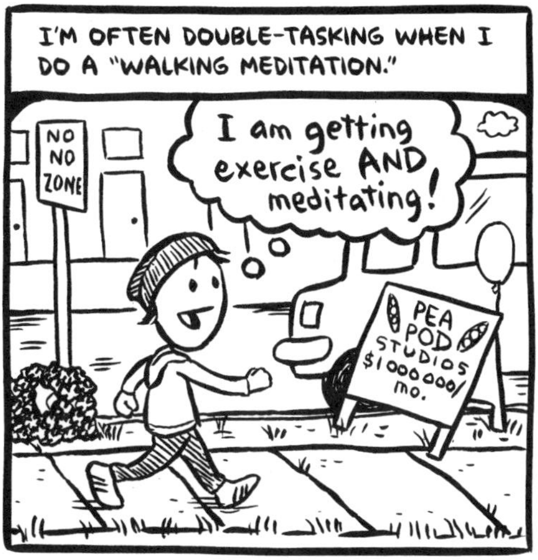
I'M OFTEN DOUBLE-TASKING WHEN I DO A "WALKING MEDITATION."
NO NO ZONE
I am getting exercise AND meditating!
PEA POD STUDIOS $1000000/mo.

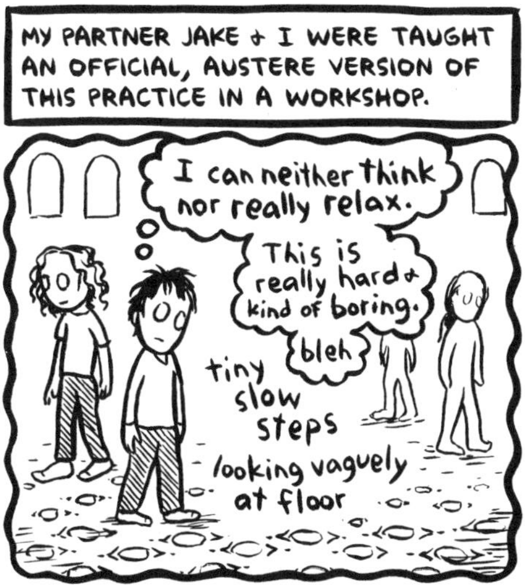
MY PARTNER JAKE & I WERE TAUGHT AN OFFICIAL, AUSTERE VERSION OF THIS PRACTICE IN A WORKSHOP.
I can neither think nor really relax.
This is really hard & kind of boring.
bleh
tiny slow steps
looking vaguely at floor

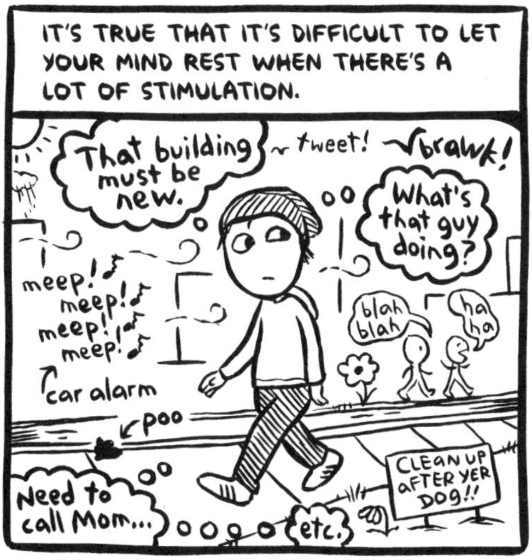
IT'S TRUE THAT IT'S DIFFICULT TO LET YOUR MIND REST WHEN THERE'S A LOT OF STIMULATION.
That building must be new.
tweet!
brawk!
What's that guy doing?
meep! meep! meep! meep!
car alarm
blah blah
ha ha
poo
Need to call Mom...
etc.
CLEAN UP AFTER YER DOG!!

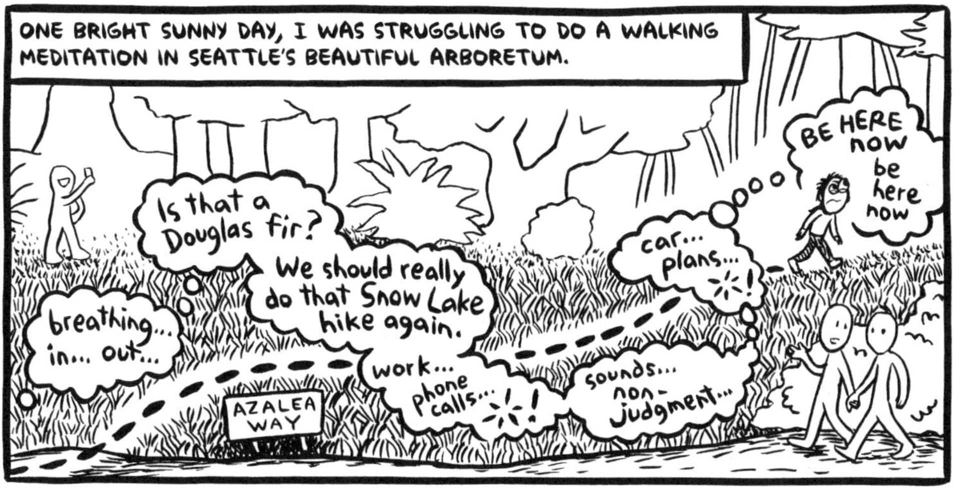
ONE BRIGHT SUNNY DAY, I WAS STRUGGLING TO DO A WALKING MEDITATION IN SEATTLE'S BEAUTIFUL ARBORETUM.
Is that a Douglas fir?
We should really do that Snow Lake hike again.
breathing... in... out...
AZALEA WAY
work... phone calls...
sounds... non-judgment...
car... plans...
BE HERE now be here now

SOMETIMES WHEN I'M MEDITATING, I PICTURE MYSELF AS PERMEABLE LIKE THIS & LET SENSATIONS JUST DRIFT THROUGH MY MIND. SO THIS STORY WAS USEFUL AFTER ALL!

⭐ THINGS THAT ARE (OR ARE LIKE) YOUR (OR SOME OTHER) THERAPY

● MAKE LISTS.

BRAIN SWIRLING?
CATCH IT.
WRITE IT DOWN.
PIN IT DOWN.

IF YOU TAKE TO THE CBT EXERCISES, DO ONE OF THOSE.

GOAL-SETTING WORKSHEET
GOAL
TARGET DATE
HOW TO REACH
HOW TO STICK TO
REACHED

laundry
refill Rx
email triage
gym
Jim
Jam
bills
laundry

> THESE ARE GREAT BECAUSE THEY TRANSFORM A SWIRLING MESS INTO NEAT PACKETS OF INFORMATION.

● MAKE CHARTS.
(MORE ON THIS IN CHAPTER 6)

SLEEP

PATTERNS

THINGS TO DO

UPS

DOWNS

Date	Hrs Sleep	Food	Mood
5-1	5½ ??	fine	anxious
5-2	7	fine	oy vey

● TAKE YOUR PRN
("AS NEEDED") MEDS.

BE CAREFUL THOUGH... THEY CAN MAKE YOU GROGGY & CAN BE PHYSICALLY OR PSYCHOLOGICALLY ADDICTIVE IF YOU TURN TO THEM A LOT. BUT I MEAN, THIS IS WHAT SOME OF THEM ARE FOR (.25 MG CLONAZEPAM FOR ME ON OCCASION) SO USE YOUR (& YOUR DOCTOR'S) JUDGMENT.

 **MANTRAS** CAN HELP PROTECT US WHEN NEGATIVE MESSAGES ARE PRESSING IN.

IT'S HELPFUL TO HAVE ONE OR AN ARRAY OF THESE.

REPEAT IT IN YOUR HEAD OR PUT IT ON A POST-IT.

(THESE ARE ALL TRIED & TRUE – FROM INTERVIEWS & MY OWN.)

You got this.

One thing at a time.

Step by step.

Anicca

SANSKRIT FOR "IMPERMANENCE" (AH-NEE-CHA)

Moment by moment.

Give it = 3 = days.

I have a 100% record of getting through the shitty times.

In this very moment... I'm okay. I'm here.

You didn't put it there, but you gotta clean it up anyway.

Let yourself off the hook.

I am worthy of love & respect.

Good enough is good enough.

The only thing you can count on is change.
One door closes, another door opens.

CUSTOMIZE FOR ANY SITUATION.

It is not my responsibility to make everyone happy.

GIVE YOURSELF A BREAK WITH SOME
LIGHT ENTERTAINMENT

ESCAPE FOR A BIT WITH A STORY YOU CAN GET LOST IN. REVISIT
FAVORITES, LOOK FOR PREDICTIBLY COMFORT-FOOD-LIKE FARE,
OR ASK FRIENDS WITH SIMILAR TASTE FOR RECOMMENDATIONS.

PERHAPS A COMFORTING STORY FOR YOU MEANS "CLASSIC HORROR
COMICS" OR "ANYTHING JOHN HUGHES OR JOHN WATERS." GO WITH
WHATEVER FEELS LIKE A SAFE, RELAXING VACATION FOR YOUR BRAIN.

LISTEN TO **MUSIC!**

MUSIC LIGHTS UP MANY DIFFERENT PARTS OF YOUR BRAIN, & CAN HAVE A SIGNIFICANT EFFECT ON MOOD.

I INTERVIEWED A BUNCH OF PEOPLE ABOUT MUSIC THEY LISTEN TO FOR HELPING WITH THEIR MOODS, & PUT TOGETHER A PLAYLIST.

WHEN I WAS WORKING ON **ROCK STEADY**, I LISTENED TO IT A LOT.

I EXPANDED THE LIST WITH MY OWN SELECTIONS, SONGS BY MUSICIANS WITH MOOD DISORDERS, KEXP'S "MUSIC HEALS: MENTAL HEALTH," & "THE HILARIOUS WORLD OF DEPRESSION" PODCAST EPISODES ABOUT MUSIC.

SOME EXCERPTS FROM

MOOD SWING,

THE **ROCK STEADY** PLAYLISTS!

Ⓐ ROCK STEADY MIXTAPE Ⓑ → **#1**

This Must Be the Place	Raccoon Cat
-Talking Heads	-Bill Frisell
Sunrise	Here Comes the Sun
-Norah Jones	-The Beatles
Dance Me to the End of Love	You've Made Me So Very Happy
-Madeleine Peyroux	-Lou Rawls
Rhiannon	Appletree
-Fleetwood Mac	-Erykah Badu
Straighten Up & Fly Right	That's the Way Love Goes
-Diana Krall	-Janet Jackson

LIFT IT UP

GENTLY UPBEAT (GET UP FROM SLEEPING OR A LOW PLACE)

MOVIN' FORWARD, CRUISIN', ONNIT.

Ⓐ ROCK STEADY MIXTAPE Ⓑ → #2

Ramble On	
- Led Zeppelin	Secrets
Keep Your Eyes Ahead	- Mary Lambert
- The Helio Sequence	The Greatest
Gooey	- Sia
- Glass Animals	Learn To Let Go
i	- Kesha
- Kendrick Lamar	Good Times
Shake It Off	- CHIC
- Taylor Swift	Could You Be Loved
	- Bob Marley & the Wailers

→ WALK RIGHT ON ～→

COMFORTING, IN A "GAAAH, MOODZ!!" KIND OF WAY

Ⓐ ROCK STEADY MIXTAPE Ⓑ → #3

Wounds	
- Kid Cudi	Sweedeedee
Amy aka Spent Gladiator 1	- Cat Power
- The Mountain Goats	Pink Cashmere
Second Skin	- Prince
- The Gits	The Weight
April Holeso	- The Band
- The Dt's	In the Waiting Line
My God Is the Sun	- Zero 7
- Queens of the Stone Age	Jetstream
	- Lusine

KICK IN THE PANTS \ SET ON DOWN

PRETTY MELLOW ↗

GRAB FROM THESE LISTS, MAKE YOUR OWN PLAYLISTS, HAVE SOME MUSIC QUEUED UP FOR WHEN YOU NEED A PICK-UP OR A CALM-DOWN.

CRYING & NOT CRYING

CRYING IS OFTEN GOOD, EVEN GREAT — CLEANSING, CALMING, CATHARTIC. BUT IT CAN BACKFIRE & MAKE YOU FEEL WORSE, IF IT'S THE WRONG CONTEXT OR IF YOU'RE GETTING PULLED INTO A CRYING SPIRAL.

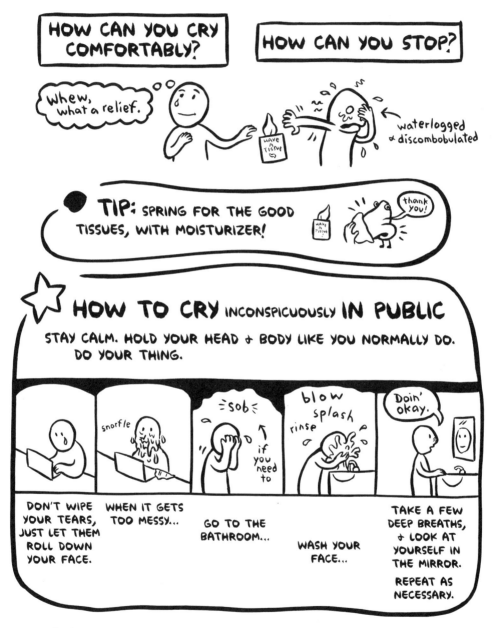

HOW CAN YOU CRY COMFORTABLY?

HOW CAN YOU STOP?

Whew, what a relief.

HAVE A TISSUE

waterlogged & discombobulated

TIP: SPRING FOR THE GOOD TISSUES, WITH MOISTURIZER!

HAVE A TISSUE

thank you!

⭐ HOW TO CRY INCONSPICUOUSLY IN PUBLIC

STAY CALM. HOLD YOUR HEAD & BODY LIKE YOU NORMALLY DO. DO YOUR THING.

snorfle

≈sob≈

if you need to

blow splash rinse

Doin' okay.

DON'T WIPE YOUR TEARS, JUST LET THEM ROLL DOWN YOUR FACE.

WHEN IT GETS TOO MESSY...

GO TO THE BATHROOM...

WASH YOUR FACE...

TAKE A FEW DEEP BREATHS, & LOOK AT YOURSELF IN THE MIRROR.

REPEAT AS NECESSARY.

NONCHALANCE WORKS IN MANY CONTEXTS — WALKING, AT A SHOW, IN CLASS — IF YOU DON'T HAVE TO INTERACT MUCH WITH ANYONE.

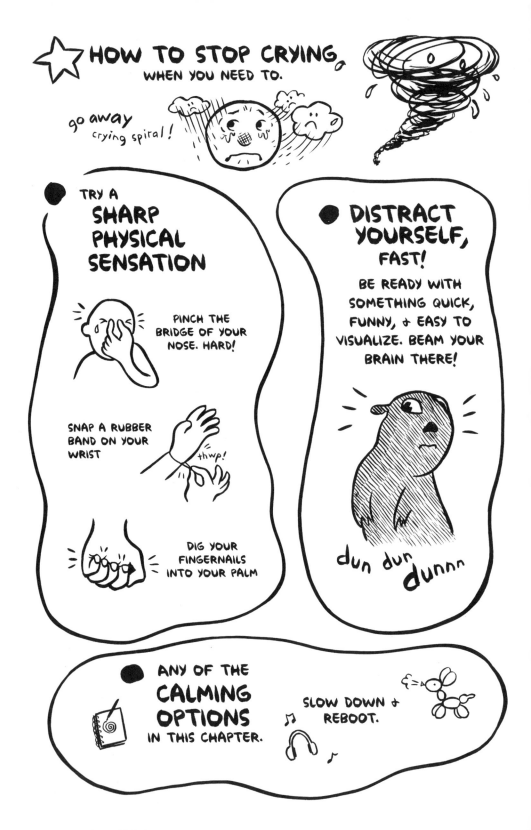

HOW TO STOP CRYING,
WHEN YOU NEED TO.

go away crying spiral!

TRY A SHARP PHYSICAL SENSATION

PINCH THE BRIDGE OF YOUR NOSE. HARD!

SNAP A RUBBER BAND ON YOUR WRIST

thwp!

DIG YOUR FINGERNAILS INTO YOUR PALM

DISTRACT YOURSELF, FAST!

BE READY WITH SOMETHING QUICK, FUNNY, & EASY TO VISUALIZE. BEAM YOUR BRAIN THERE!

dun dun dunnn

ANY OF THE CALMING OPTIONS IN THIS CHAPTER.

SLOW DOWN & REBOOT.

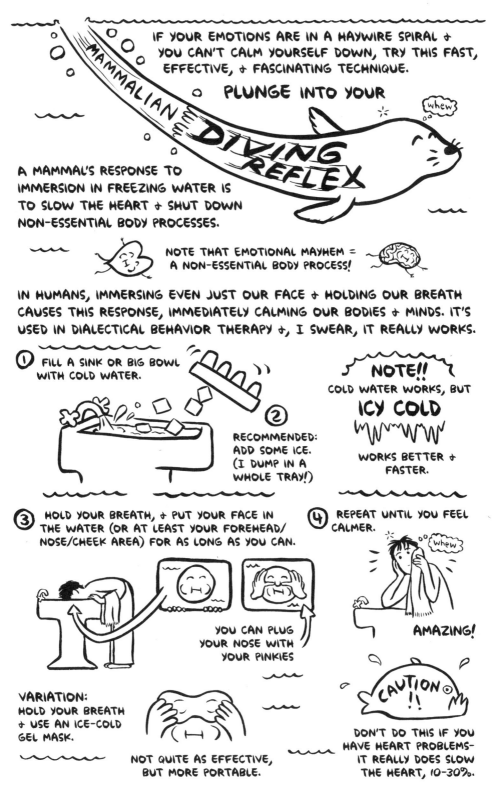

IF YOUR EMOTIONS ARE IN A HAYWIRE SPIRAL & YOU CAN'T CALM YOURSELF DOWN, TRY THIS FAST, EFFECTIVE, & FASCINATING TECHNIQUE.

PLUNGE INTO YOUR

MAMMALIAN DIVING REFLEX

whew

A MAMMAL'S RESPONSE TO IMMERSION IN FREEZING WATER IS TO SLOW THE HEART & SHUT DOWN NON-ESSENTIAL BODY PROCESSES.

NOTE THAT EMOTIONAL MAYHEM = A NON-ESSENTIAL BODY PROCESS!

IN HUMANS, IMMERSING EVEN JUST OUR FACE & HOLDING OUR BREATH CAUSES THIS RESPONSE, IMMEDIATELY CALMING OUR BODIES & MINDS. IT'S USED IN DIALECTICAL BEHAVIOR THERAPY &, I SWEAR, IT REALLY WORKS.

① FILL A SINK OR BIG BOWL WITH COLD WATER.

② RECOMMENDED: ADD SOME ICE. (I DUMP IN A WHOLE TRAY!)

NOTE!!
COLD WATER WORKS, BUT
ICY COLD
WORKS BETTER & FASTER.

③ HOLD YOUR BREATH, & PUT YOUR FACE IN THE WATER (OR AT LEAST YOUR FOREHEAD/ NOSE/CHEEK AREA) FOR AS LONG AS YOU CAN.

YOU CAN PLUG YOUR NOSE WITH YOUR PINKIES

④ REPEAT UNTIL YOU FEEL CALMER.

whew

AMAZING!

VARIATION: HOLD YOUR BREATH & USE AN ICE-COLD GEL MASK.

NOT QUITE AS EFFECTIVE, BUT MORE PORTABLE.

CAUTION!!

DON'T DO THIS IF YOU HAVE HEART PROBLEMS— IT REALLY DOES SLOW THE HEART, 10-30%.

GOING OUT & STAYING IN

IT'S IMPORTANT TO NURTURE YOURSELF QUIETLY AT HOME, BUT JUST AS IMPORTANT NOT TO ISOLATE YOURSELF.

OH, HOW I WOULD AGONIZE OVER THIS WHEN I WAS DOWN.

The glass is half-empty no matter what I do!

● **MAINTAIN A BALANCE** BETWEEN LETTING YOURSELF STAY HOME & GATHERING YOUR ENERGY TO GO OUT. SOMETIMES YOU WILL GO OUT & WISH YOU'D STAYED IN, & VICE VERSA. THAT'S OKAY!

REALLY STUCK? MAYBE FLIP A COIN.

heads: art walk
tails: bubble bath

● SOME QUESTIONS TO HELP YOU DECIDE IF STAYING AT HOME IS

HEALING... OR "SELF-ISOLATING":

DOES STAYING AT HOME FEEL SOOTHING...

ARE YOU DOING SOMETHING THAT FEELS LIKE CARING FOR YOURSELF (LIKE ANYTHING IN CHAPTER 3)...

IS IT RARE THAT YOU HAVE SOME SOLITUDE?

ARE YOU SICK WITH A COLD?

HAVE YOU BEEN SOCIAL & JUST NEED A BREAK?

...OR DO YOU WIND UP FEELING DOWN ON YOURSELF?

...OR PUTTERING ANXIOUSLY, FLIPPING THROUGH JUNK MAIL, OR CURLING UP IN A BALL UNDER A BLANKET?

ARE YOU TURNING TO THE INTERNET INSTEAD OF YOUR PEOPLE?

HAVE YOU STAYED AT HOME OR IN BED FOR DAYS?

ARE YOU AVOIDING ANSWERING THE PHONE?

DO YOU FEEL LIKE NO ONE LIKES YOU?

GO THROUGH THE MOTIONS.

THINK: WHAT DID YOU DO WHEN YOU FELT OKAY? WALK YOURSELF THROUGH THOSE FAMILIAR STEPS, & THE FEEDBACK LOOP INSIDE YOU & WITH OTHER PEOPLE & THE ENVIRONMENT MAY KICK YOU INTO GEAR.

I don't know how to dress myself.

WEAR SOMETHING YOU HAVE A MEMORY (OR A PHOTO) OF FEELING GOOD IN, & DON'T LOOK IN THE MIRROR AGAIN.

(IF YOU REALLY HAVE NO IDEA, JUST WEAR SOMETHING COMFORTABLE & ALL BLACK.)

FOLLOW YOUR OWN SCRIPT.

I am going to the kitchen.

YOU KNOW HOW TO WALK ACROSS THE ROOM

& SAY CERTAIN THINGS

Thanks

Totally

What's up with you?

MAYBE THE OTHER PERSON CAN CARRY THE CONVERSATION

I can do this, actually.

& LISTEN

hm

Am I being boring? NO!
YOU ARE NOT.

BE QUIET IF YOU WANT TO.

YOU DON'T NEED TO BE TALKATIVE OR ENTERTAINING! THINK OF YOURSELF AS RESERVED & MYSTERIOUS, IF THAT HELPS.

● LEAVE WHEN YOU NEED TO.

IF A WHOLE NIGHT OUT SOUNDS EXHAUSTING, KNOW
THAT YOU CAN GO OUT & THEN CHANGE YOUR MIND.

OR JUST PLAN TO GO OUT
FOR AN HOUR.

ONE LOW-PRESSURE WAY TO GO OUT IS TO
● DO SOMETHING RELATIVELY PASSIVE,

LIKE READING AT A COFFEE SHOP OR
SEEING A PLAY OR A MOVIE.

MAYBE WITH A FRIEND WHO
KNOWS YOU'RE FEELING LOW,
& YOU CAN BE QUIET TOGETHER.

MAYBE JUST BY YOURSELF, FOR A HANDLEABLE
MIDDLE GROUND BETWEEN SOCIALIZING & SOLITUDE.

JUST AS IMPORTANT AS TAKING CARE OF YOURSELF, **YOURSELF,**

REACH OUT TO OTHER PEOPLE --

--A SUPPORT GROUP NEAR YOU, AN ONLINE MESSAGE BOARD, A PHONE LINE--

-- & ESPECIALLY,
REACH OUT TO YOUR TEAM, YOUR SUPPORT SYSTEM.

CALL YOUR MOM. TEXT YOUR FRIEND.

ASK YOUR PARTNER FOR SOME EXTRA SUPPORT.

ASK YOUR BEST FRIEND TO TEXT EVERY ONCE IN A WHILE THAT SHE LOVES YOU.

GET A GOOD SOLID HUG.

GET SOME PERSPECTIVE.

THERE'S SO MUCH WE CAN DO – BUT WE CAN'T DO IT **ALL** BY OURSELVES.

MERIT BADGES
FOR USING OR DEVELOPING
TOOLS THAT ARE

EASY

CONVENIENT

ENTERTAINING

CREATIVE

PHYSICAL

MEDITATIVE *
MINDFUL

SELF-
COMPASSIONATE

COMFORTING

OUTREACHING

CHAPTER 4
INSOMNIA

INSOMNIA IS **CRUEL**.

SLEEP IS OUR #1 PRIORITY, SO
HOW CAN IT BE SO **EVASIVE?!**

poot!

ha ha ha ha!

ha ha ha!!

← HARRASS

← HOVER

no no no

CREEP →

**INSOMNIA
MONSTERS**

IT'S GOOD TO HAVE MANY OPTIONS FOR DIFFERENT
SITUATIONS & SLEEP PATTERNS. MIX & MATCH!

SOME GENERAL SLEEPING TIPS

- AS MUCH AS POSSIBLE, ONLY USE YOUR BED FOR **SLEEPING & SEX.**

  GO SOMEWHERE ELSE TO WATCH TV, EAT BREAKFAST, OR READ (OR HAVE SEX, FOR THAT MATTER, PERHAPS).

  Z^Z

- **WATCH YOUR SUBSTANCES**

  AVOID **CAFFEINE** LATE IN THE DAY. FIGURE OUT YOUR CUT-OFF TIME.

  GREEN TEA   DECAF COFFEE!   SODA

  WATCH FOR SNEAKY SOURCES OF CAFFEINE, TOO, INCLUDING:

  CHOCOLATE   ICE CREAM   ENERGY WATER

  TRUE FACT:

  ALCOHOL & POT DON'T HELP YOU SLEEP. THEY MAY KNOCK YOU OUT, BUT YOU DON'T GET GOOD QUALITY SLEEP. (MORE ON SUBSTANCES IN CHAPTER 6.)

- DO WHAT YOU CAN TO **STICK TO YOUR REGULAR SLEEP SCHEDULE**

  Can we go to an earlier show? That's past my bedtime.

  Earlier won't be 3-D

  Well uh. Did I tell you 3-D gives me gas? ☺

  Early show it is!!

- AVOID **ALL-NIGHTERS**

  RED-EYE FLIGHTS, STUDYING MARATHONS, NIGHT SHIFTS.

GOOD WAKEFULNESS & GOOD SLEEP GO HAND IN HAND.

GET SOME **LIGHT** DURING THE DAY...

...**SUNLIGHT**, IDEALLY!

GET SOME OF NATURE'S COLOR SPECTRUM. TAKE A WALK OUTSIDE IN THE MORNING, OR AT LUNCHTIME, OR WHENEVER YOU CAN.

SO nice!

BRIGHT LIGHT THERAPY LAMPS CAN WORK WELL FOR DEPRESSION FOR SOME PEOPLE

(BUT CAN TRIGGER MANIA FOR OTHERS, SO BE CAREFUL).

IN WINTER, **LIGHT A CANDLE** AROUND DUSK.

BEESWAX IS GREAT

A NOTE ON **NAPS** A TRADEOFF: THEY CAN MESS WITH YOUR NIGHTTIME SLEEPING, BUT CAN ALSO HELP WITH SLEEP EQUILIBRIUM OVER THE WHOLE DAY.

PERSONALLY, I LOVE NAPS - BUT IT'S IMPORTANT TO KEEP THEM SHORT, 10-20 MINS.

PERHAPS THAT SOUNDS AWFULLY SHORT. THINK OF IT AS A "CAT NAP" OR "POWER NAP," WHICHEVER SOUNDS MORE APPEALING!

☆ GOING TO BED

● HAVE A
BEDTIME RITUAL

SOMETHING TO HELP SIGNAL THAT IT'S
TIME TO SAY GOODBYE TO THE DAY.

A PARTICULAR SONG

♪Sweedee dee...

NIGHTLY PERSONAL CARE

OVERNIGHT FACE MASQUE

FLOSS AT END OF DAY

ENTRY IN MOOD CHART

● **LIMIT YOUR SCREENS** IN THE EVENING,
ESPECIALLY IN THE HOUR BEFORE BEDTIME.

Staay awaaake...awaaaake...

ASIDE FROM THE STRESS OF SOCIAL MEDIA – !! – THE
BLUE LIGHT FROM SCREENS MIMICS DAYLIGHT, WHICH
CONFUSES OUR CIRCADIAN RHYTHMS & KEEPS OUR
BRAINS & BODIES FROM WINDING DOWN.

IF SETTING THEM ASIDE ISN'T AN OPTION, THERE ARE:

BLUE-BLOCKING GLASSES

SCREEN FILTERS

orangey

APPS THAT ADJUST YOUR SCREEN'S COLORS.

USE THE LIGHTS

DIM OR TURN THEM OFF

click!

TURN ON YOUR BEDSIDE LAMP AS YOU GET READY FOR BED, SO IT'S AN INVITING SPOT.

SO COMFY IN THERE!

THE OL' VIPARITA KARANI

WHICH IS SANSKRIT FOR THIS EASY, RESTORATIVE YOGA POSE.

LIE WITH YOUR LEGS UP THE WALL FOR 5 OR 10 MINUTES.

BREATHE

PRESCRIPTION SLEEP MEDS

IF YOU NEED SOME EXTRA HELP, SLEEP MEDS CAN BE A GOOD TOOL. BUT! BE CAREFUL — MANY OF THEM ARE ADDICTIVE (INCLUDING CLONAZAPAM & OTHER BENZODIAZEPINES) SO IF POSSIBLE, DON'T USE THEM EVERY NIGHT FOR THE LONG TERM.

Take 2 for ZZZ

(AFTER SOME POINT, IT'S HARD TO SLEEP WITHOUT THEM, THEN YOU NEED MORE & MORE TO WORK, & THEIR EFFECTIVENESS GOES DOWN & DOWN. THEN GETTING OFF THEM IS AN ORDEAL, & IT'S JUST A BIG DRAG.)

THERE ARE MANY OVER THE COUNTER PRODUCTS

SOME WORK, SOME DON'T. RESEARCH, GET RECOMMENDATIONS, TRY THINGS... JUST **CHECK WITH YOUR DOCTOR** TO MAKE SURE THEY WON'T MESS WITH YOUR REGULAR MEDS OR MAKE YOU DEPRESSED!

IF YOU ARE MANIC & HAVING TROUBLE WINDING DOWN, OR IF YOU'RE HAVING TROUBLE EVEN WANTING TO WIND DOWN--

JUST
● TAKE YOUR SLEEPING MED.

IT WILL TAKE 20 SECONDS. (I TIMED IT.)

IT'S REALLY HARD TO MAKE YOURSELF GO TO SLEEP WHEN YOU'RE MANIC. BUT YOU HAVE TO SLEEP.

YOU DON'T HAVE TO GO TO BED YET...

JUST THINK OF THE QUEEN & SWALLOW.

SOON...

Bed actually sounds pretty good.

... IT WILL DO THE REST OF THE WINDING-DOWN WORK.

☆ GOING TO SLEEP

A MEDITATION PRACTICE IS REALLY, REALLY USEFUL HERE, TO HELP YOUR THOUGHTS & BODY SLOW DOWN & LET GO.

● LISTEN TO A GUIDED SLEEP MEDITATION

THERE ARE FREE ONES ONLINE, & OF COURSE APPS & NUMEROUS AUDIO FORMATS. LISTENING TO SOMEONE ELSE'S VOICE CAN HELP A LOT WHEN IT'S DIFFICULT TO FOCUS.

Allow thinking to dissolve into sensing...

JENNIFER PIERCY'S "HEALING DARKNESS FOR SLEEP" ON THE INSIGHT TIMER APP KNOCKS ME OUT EVERY TIME.

See if you can find a position that's 10% more comfortable...

Feel your body relax & sink into the mattress...

● LISTEN TO A PODCAST

BORING IS GOOD!

Today on the Watching Paint Dry-cast, a St. Louis home interior stylist switches from eggshell to satin. We ask him why.

● LISTEN TO WHITE NOISE WITH A GADGET, APP, ONLINE, OR OTHER AUDIO SOURCE.

AT HOME I AM LULLED BY THE SOUND OF THE DISHWASHER.

chugga chugga chugga chugga

ONE TIME, TRAVELING & JET LAGGED:

Hey! This white noise app has a dishwasher sound!

chugga chugga chugga

SOON:

chugga chugga chugga chugga

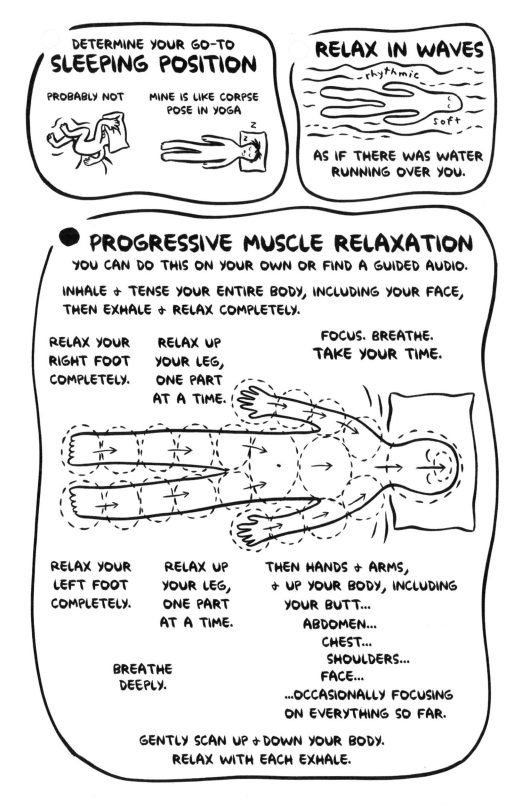

DETERMINE YOUR GO-TO
SLEEPING POSITION

PROBABLY NOT

MINE IS LIKE CORPSE
POSE IN YOGA

RELAX IN WAVES

rhythmic

soft

AS IF THERE WAS WATER
RUNNING OVER YOU.

● PROGRESSIVE MUSCLE RELAXATION
YOU CAN DO THIS ON YOUR OWN OR FIND A GUIDED AUDIO.

INHALE & TENSE YOUR ENTIRE BODY, INCLUDING YOUR FACE,
THEN EXHALE & RELAX COMPLETELY.

RELAX YOUR
RIGHT FOOT
COMPLETELY.

RELAX UP
YOUR LEG,
ONE PART
AT A TIME.

FOCUS. BREATHE.
TAKE YOUR TIME.

RELAX YOUR
LEFT FOOT
COMPLETELY.

RELAX UP
YOUR LEG,
ONE PART
AT A TIME.

THEN HANDS & ARMS,
& UP YOUR BODY, INCLUDING
YOUR BUTT...
ABDOMEN...
CHEST...
SHOULDERS...
FACE...
...OCCASIONALLY FOCUSING
ON EVERYTHING SO FAR.

BREATHE
DEEPLY.

GENTLY SCAN UP & DOWN YOUR BODY.
RELAX WITH EACH EXHALE.

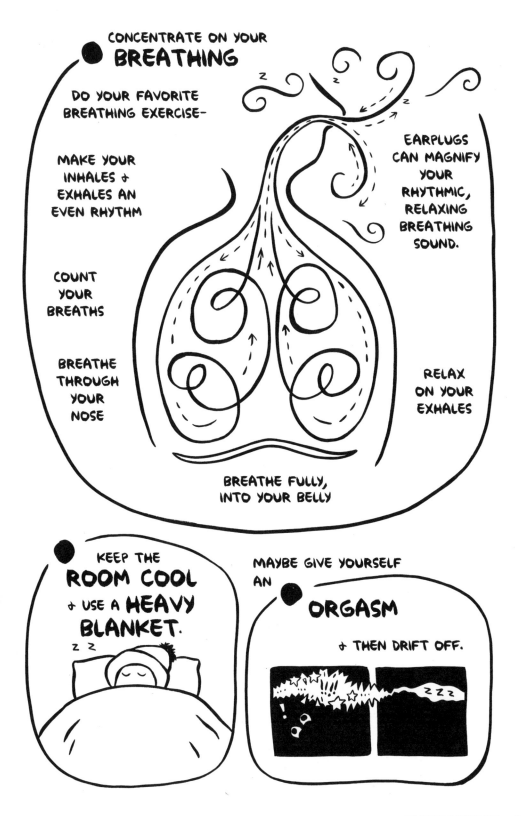

CONCENTRATE ON YOUR
BREATHING

DO YOUR FAVORITE
BREATHING EXERCISE—

MAKE YOUR
INHALES &
EXHALES AN
EVEN RHYTHM

EARPLUGS
CAN MAGNIFY
YOUR
RHYTHMIC,
RELAXING
BREATHING
SOUND.

COUNT
YOUR
BREATHS

BREATHE
THROUGH
YOUR
NOSE

RELAX
ON YOUR
EXHALES

BREATHE FULLY,
INTO YOUR BELLY

KEEP THE
ROOM COOL
& USE A **HEAVY BLANKET.**
z z

MAYBE GIVE YOURSELF
AN
ORGASM

& THEN DRIFT OFF.

MIND YOUR SENSES

USE AN EYE MASK

Princess — SASSY

CUPS DON'T SQUISH EYEBALLS

SILK ON ONE SIDE, TERRY ON THE OTHER

OR AN EYE PILLOW

PLAIN

FANCY

FILLED WITH LAVENDER

TENT A PILLOW OVER YOUR HEAD TO BLOCK SOUND & LIGHT.

TUCK

USE EARPLUGS

A FAVORITE SMELL: LAVENDER IS GENERALLY THE RECOMMENDED SLEEPY AROMATHERAPY.

(BUT TRY WHATEVER WORKS FOR YOU.

SAWDUST = CHILDHOOD TOYS?)

A HOT WATER BOTTLE CAN WARM COLD FEET

IT'S HARD TO SLEEP WITH COLD FEET — I KNOW THIS WELL!

⭐ WAKING UP IN THE MIDDLE OF THE NIGHT

MY PERSONAL BIGGEST SLEEP BATTLE.

IF YOU'VE BEEN AWAKE FOR AT LEAST 20 MINUTES, **ACCEPT THAT YOU ARE IN FACT AWAKE.** TOSSING & TURNING & FRUSTRATION WILL NOT BRING YOU SLEEP.

SOMETIMES I WAKE UP WITH SWIRLING THOUGHTS & IT FEELS SOMEHOW IMPORTANT TO WRESTLE WITH THEM RIGHT THEN.

I HAVE TO REMIND MYSELF THAT MY GOAL RIGHT THEN – MY **JOB** – IS TO SLEEP.

COMMIT TO SLEEPING.

must sleep sleepsleepsleep sleepsleep..shit!
what was..?
must
don't forget to ???
guilt ₹₹₹ fear no
stupid
I can't? ???
tomorrow
I wonder when..
yesterday
frustration
anxiety
did I -?
too late for sleep med
obsess
should have could have
too early to get up
relax relax relax relax relax relax ..shit!
what if but
can't stop need to

DON'T KEEP LOOKING AT THE CLOCK!

THE SILENT STARE OF THE WEE HOURS CLOCK MONSTER

YOU MIGHT TAKE A SLEEP MED IF IT'S STILL EARLY ENOUGH IN THE NIGHT.

● KEEP A JOURNAL BY YOUR BED (& CONVENIENT PEN) SO YOU CAN:

WRITE DOWN THAT AWESOME IDEA...

WRITE DOWN THAT THING YOU DON'T WANT TO FORGET...

WRITE A LIST OF THE THINGS SWIRLING IN YOUR HEAD...

(BECAUSE AWESOME IDEAS DO SOMETIMES COME IN THE MIDDLE OF THE NIGHT)

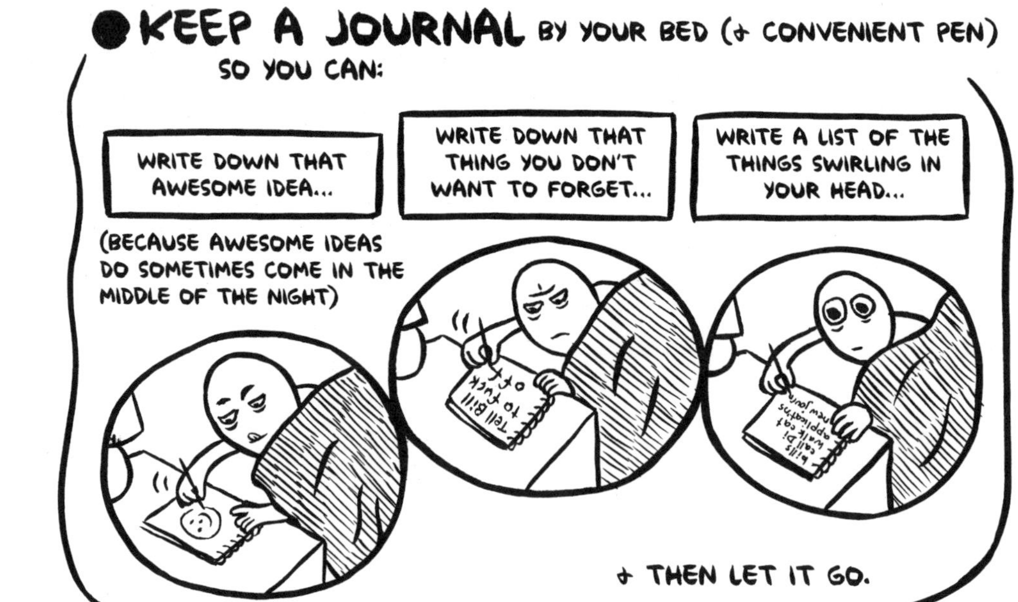
Tell Bill to fuck off

& THEN LET IT GO.

● REBOOT SOMEHOW.

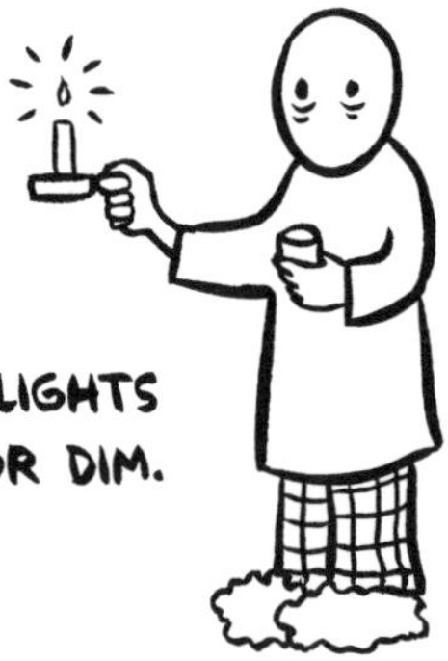

- GET UP IF YOU'VE BEEN AWAKE FOR AT LEAST 20 MINUTES.
- KEEP LIGHTS OFF OR DIM.
- AVOID SCREENS - PHONE, LAPTOP, GADGETS.

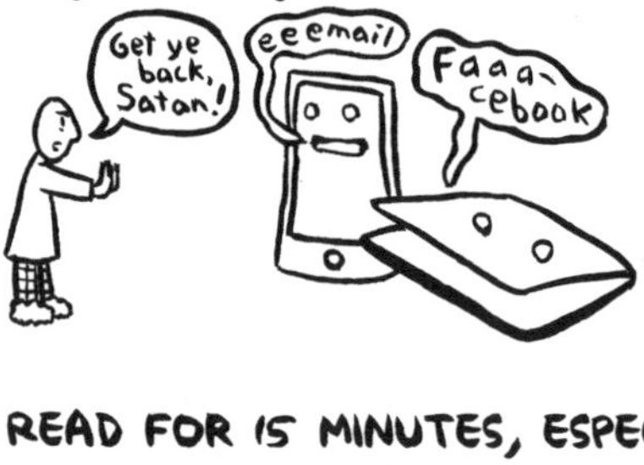
Get ye back, Satan!
eeemail
Faaa-cebook

- EAT A TINY BIT, MAYBE CEREAL, OR HAVE SOME WARM MILK OR SLEEPY TEA.
- READ FOR 15 MINUTES, ESPECIALLY SOMETHING REALLY SHORT OR KIND OF BORING.

RESTAURANTS REVIEWS IN A FAR-AWAY CITY

MOVIE LISTINGS ARE LIKE VERY SHORT STORIES

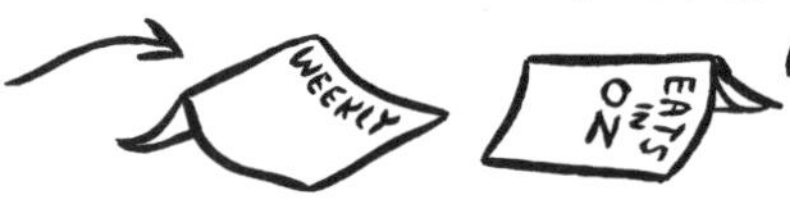
WEEKLY

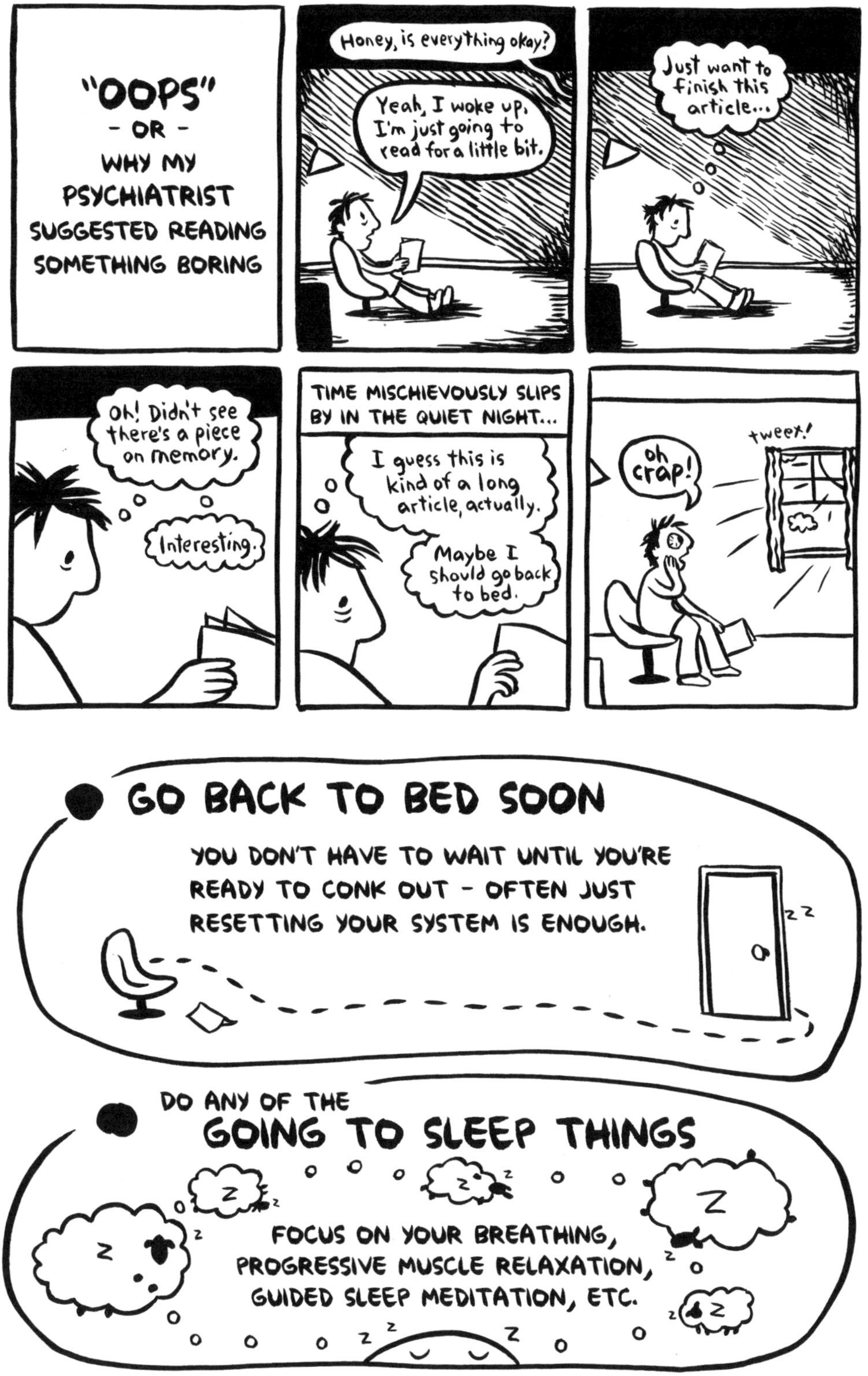
"OOPS"
- OR -
WHY MY PSYCHIATRIST SUGGESTED READING SOMETHING BORING
Honey, is everything okay?
Yeah, I woke up. I'm just going to read for a little bit.
Just want to finish this article...
Oh! Didn't see there's a piece on memory.
Interesting.
TIME MISCHIEVOUSLY SLIPS BY IN THE QUIET NIGHT...
I guess this is kind of a long article, actually.
Maybe I should go back to bed.
oh crap!
tweet!
GO BACK TO BED SOON
YOU DON'T HAVE TO WAIT UNTIL YOU'RE READY TO CONK OUT - OFTEN JUST RESETTING YOUR SYSTEM IS ENOUGH.
DO ANY OF THE GOING TO SLEEP THINGS
FOCUS ON YOUR BREATHING, PROGRESSIVE MUSCLE RELAXATION, GUIDED SLEEP MEDITATION, ETC.

TRAVEL MEANS CHANGES IN YOUR ROUTINE & FINELY TUNED CIRCADIAN RHYTHMS, EVEN IF YOU DON'T CROSS TIME ZONES. BUT WHEN YOU DO CHANGE TIME ZONES: UGGGH, JET LAG CAN HIT HARD.

☆ DEALING WITH JET LAG

● GET INTO THE NEW TIME ZONE AS SOON AS YOU CAN.

– OR –

● IF YOU'RE ONLY THERE FOR A SHORT TIME, YOU COULD TRY STICKING TO YOUR HOME TIME ZONE SCHEDULE.

● GET SOME DAYLIGHT IN THE MORNING.

● A NAP UP TO AN HOUR ON THE FIRST DAY IS OKAY, BUT IN GENERAL, AVOID LONG NAPS.

● SOME EASY PHYSICAL EXERCISE HELPS A LOT.

AND THEN ON THE OTHER SIDE OF THE BED, THERE'S

HYPERSOMNIA.

DEPRESSION MAKES US WANT TO SLEEP SO BAD, PARTLY FOR THE ESCAPE AND PARTLY BECAUSE WE'RE JUST EXHAUSTED.

BUT AS MUCH AS YOU CAN, GET UP & OUT OF BED IN THE MORNING, & KEEP YOURSELF AWAKE DURING THE DAY.

IF YOU DO NAP, MAKE IT SHORT – & GET BACK UP. TURN ON LIGHTS, PUT ON MUSIC, GET YOUR HEART RATE UP EVEN JUST A TINY BIT. GO OUTSIDE OR EVEN JUST WALK ACROSS THE ROOM & STRETCH.

REMIND YOURSELF THAT BEING UP DURING THE DAY WILL INCREASE YOUR CHANCES OF A GOOD SLEEP AT NIGHT.

REMIND YOURSELF THAT DEPRESSION ENDS & YOU WON'T BE EXHAUSTED FOREVER.

MERIT BADGES FOR
INSOMNIA

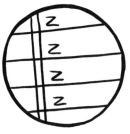

REGULAR SLEEP
SCHEDULE

↑ SUNLIGHT

IXNAY SCREENS

GOING TO SLEEP

GOING BACK
TO SLEEP

STAYING ASLEEP

JET LAG

SHORT NAP

AVOIDING
OVERSLEEPING

CHAPTER 5
DEALING WITH
MEDS

WHO REALLY WANTS TO TAKE MEDS?

NEED 'EM!
DON'T NEED 'EM!
WRONG ONES!
RIGHT ONES!
SIDE EFFECTS!

ON 'EM!
OFF 'EM!
LOVE 'EM!
HATE 'EM!
FORGET TO TAKE 'EM!

KNOW THIS: **TAKING MEDS IS NOT WEAK.** IT CAN – BUT DOESN'T NEED TO BE – YOUR GOAL TO GET OFF MEDS.

THINK OF IT THIS WAY: IF I NEED GLASSES BECAUSE OTHERWISE I CRASH INTO THINGS, THEN I NEED TO JUST WEAR SOME FRICKIN' GLASSES.

EYE EXERCISES COULD BE ENOUGH. THAT'D BE GREAT! BUT MAYBE I JUST NEED THE GLASSES.

DETERMINING WHICH MEDS ARE APPROPRIATE & EFFECTIVE FOR YOU, IF ANY, AS SHORT- OR LONG-TERM TREATMENT, IS COMPLICATED.

THIS CHAPTER IS ABOUT INCORPORATING MEDS INTO YOUR LIFE IF YOU'VE DETERMINED THAT YOU **DO** NEED THEM TO BE HEALTHY.

DO YOU REALLY NEED MEDS ANYMORE?

WHEN MY MEMOIR WAS ABOUT TO COME OUT IN 2012, I'D BEEN STABLE FOR 10 YEARS, & WANTED SOME CONFIRMATION FROM MY DOCTOR.

MOOD DISORDERS ARE RECURRENT, SO WE HAVE TO DEAL WITH THEM OVER THE LONG HAUL, SOMEHOW. FOR MANY OF US, OUR CHANCES OF GETTING & STAYING WELL ARE MUCH GREATER WITH TREATMENT THAT INCLUDES THE RIGHT MEDICATIONS.

☆ IMPORTANT NOTE! ONE OF THE BIGGEST CAUSES OF RELAPSE IS GOING OFF MEDS TOO FAST.

☆ AT HOME

● KEEP YOUR MEDS SOMEWHERE CONVENIENT

A SHELF IN THE KITCHEN (= EASY ACCESS TO DRINKING GLASS & WATER) WORKS BETTER FOR ME THAN THE BATHROOM (= WEIRD OLD MEDICINE CABINET, NO COUNTER).

& IN SOMETHING THAT YOU LIKE.

I STILL READ THE COMICS ON MY PEANUTS LUNCHBOX & THEY STILL MAKE ME HAPPY.

● MAKE SURE YOUR MEDS ARE EASY TO IDENTIFY.

LABEL THEM ON THE TOP IF YOU KEEP THEM IN SOME SORT OF BOX, LIKE I DO.

BIRD'S EYE VIEW

LITHIUM
LAMOTRIGINE
SPIRONOLACTONE
CLONAZEPAM (KLONOPIN) PRN

GLITTERY DRAGON STICKER THAT A STUDENT GAVE ME IN A GET-WELL CARD AFTER I WAS IN A BIKE ACCIDENT.

REMEMBERING TO TAKE THEM CAN BE TRICKY,
ESPECIALLY IF YOU'RE HAVING MEMORY PROBLEMS OR IF YOUR ROUTINE GETS MESSED UP. FIND WHAT WORKS FOR YOU, & SWITCH IT UP IF YOU'RE FORGETTING AGAIN.

● USE A DAILY DISPENSER.

THE CLASSIC. I FOUND THEM KIND OF A PAIN & I'D FORGET TO ORDER REFILLS. BUT THEY'RE A POPULAR SYSTEM & CHEAP.

← TOOK

NOT YET TOOK

● FIND A PILL-REMINDER APP.

bloodle-oop!

Time to take your medication!

MEDISAFE IS ONE — IT STORES YOUR MED INFO, & YOU RECORD WHEN YOU TAKE THEM.

● SET A CUSTOM ALARM ON YOUR PHONE.

Hey beautiful! No illin', be pillin'!

Let's go crazy Let's get nuts

● WRITE YOURSELF A NOTE, & LEAVE IT WHERE YOU WILL FIND IT AT THE RIGHT TIME.

MEDS!

BRITE TOOTHZ

● TURN THEM UPSIDE DOWN WHEN YOU'VE TAKEN THEM.
MY CURRENT LOW-IMPACT TRACKING METHOD.

READY TO TAKE IN AM

PUT AWAY LIKE THIS

READY TO TAKE IN PM

PUT AWAY LIKE THIS

● DON'T FREAK OUT IF YOU MISS A DOSE!

DON'T DOUBLE UP, JUST MAKE SURE TO TAKE YOUR NEXT ONE.

IF THIS HAPPENS OFTEN, THOUGH, TRY A NEW STRATEGY!

TAKING MEDS IS NOT EASY, EVEN IF YOU'RE DEDICATED & HAVE BEEN TAKING MEDS FOR YEARS. EVERYONE MESSES UP SOMETIMES.

'CUZ YOU KNOW. SHIT HAPPENS.

GENERIC TERMS

- OR -

THE TIME I ACCIDENTALLY TOOK VITAMIN D INSTEAD OF MY MOOD STABILIZER FOR THREE FULL DAYS

MY PEANUTS LUNCHBOX IS FOR MY REGULAR MEDS, & A SECOND LUNCHBOX ON A LOW SHELF IS FOR MY MOTLEY COLLECTION OF MISCELLANY.

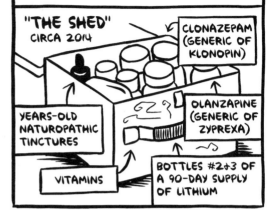

"THE SHED" CIRCA 2014

CLONAZEPAM (GENERIC OF KLONOPIN)

OLANZAPINE (GENERIC OF ZYPREXA)

YEARS-OLD NATUROPATHIC TINCTURES

VITAMINS

BOTTLES #2&3 OF A 90-DAY SUPPLY OF LITHIUM

A FEW YEARS AGO, I WAS LATE TO REFILL MY LAMOTRIGINE, & RAN OUT BEFORE THE NEW MEDS ARRIVED IN THE MAIL.

Good thing I have an auxilliary supply for just such an occasion.

UH-OH!

ACTUAL AUXILLIARY SUPPLY

POORLY LABELED TRAVEL CONTAINER

THREE DAYS LATER, I TOOK A BETTER LOOK AT THE BOTTLE.

What the--??!!?

VIT D
Rx#123
amotrigine
1 TABLET
TWICE DAILY

Is this... the bottle I took to Florida?! I've been taking vitamin D instead of my mood stabilizer?!!?!

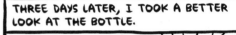

NAME BRAND LAMICTAL: ◇ blue   GENERIC LAMOTRIGINE: ○ white   VITAMIN D: ○ white

I WAS ALMOST TOO EMBARRASSED TO CALL MY DOCTOR. BUT:

!!#☆⊙!⚡

Re/starting lamotrigine too quickly increases the risk of its most notorious side effect, a fatal rash.

smak!

SHE TOLD ME TO GO AHEAD & RESTART (WITH THE CORRECT PILLS...) BUT TO STAY EXTRA ALERT FOR THE RASH.

LAM
Kl
Li
Rx#
Lamotrigi
Clonaze
EXP
TAKE I TAB
TWICE DAI
Lithium Rx#

IN THE END, EVERYTHING WAS OKAY. BUT ALL OF MY MEDS ARE VERY WELL MARKED NOW - EVEN IN THE SHED.

CUTTING PILLS

YOU MIGHT NEED TO CUT YOUR PILLS IF YOUR DOSAGE ISN'T STANDARD, OR IF YOU'RE TAPERING ON OR OFF, OR BECAUSE ONE 10MG TABLET MIGHT BE A LOT CHEAPER THAN TWO 5MG TABLETS.

● BREAK WITH YOUR
FINGERS

EVEN UNSCORED PILLS USUALLY SNAP PRETTY EASILY.

BRING THUMBNAILS TO TOUCH

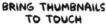

=chk=

● USE A
PILL CUTTER

I HAD ONE THAT JUST MADE MY PILLS CRUMBLE, SO I'M NOT A BIG FAN, BUT MAYBE I JUST HAD A DUD. SOME PEOPLE SWEAR BY THESE.

● TIP: IF YOU DROP A PILL ON THE FLOOR,
FIND IT & PICK IT UP!

NOTHING FEELS LIKE

weeeeee!

I am kooky tunes & just PILLS, PILLS, everywhere!!

LIKE HAVING PILLS AROUND LIKE DEBRIS.

uh oh!

?

ALSO, IF THERE ARE BABIES OR PETS AROUND, YOU DO NOT WANT THEM TO EAT YOUR MEDS!

benzo!

SWALLOWING YOUR PILLS ALL AT ONCE HAS THE DOUBLE ADVANTAGE OF MAKING TAKING MEDS QUICKER, & A SPORT!

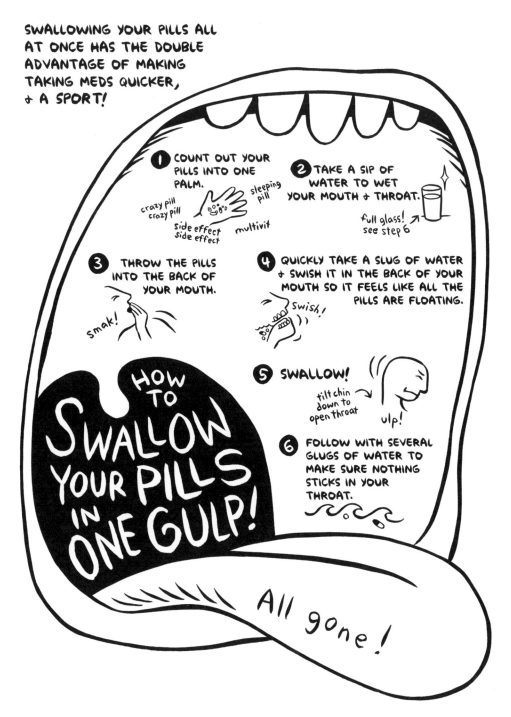

HOW TO SWALLOW YOUR PILLS IN ONE GULP!

1. COUNT OUT YOUR PILLS INTO ONE PALM.

crazy pill
crazy pill
sleeping pill
side effect
side effect
multivit

2. TAKE A SIP OF WATER TO WET YOUR MOUTH & THROAT.

full glass!
see step 6

3. THROW THE PILLS INTO THE BACK OF YOUR MOUTH.

smak!

4. QUICKLY TAKE A SLUG OF WATER & SWISH IT IN THE BACK OF YOUR MOUTH SO IT FEELS LIKE ALL THE PILLS ARE FLOATING.

swish!

5. SWALLOW!

tilt chin down to open throat

ulp!

6. FOLLOW WITH SEVERAL GLUGS OF WATER TO MAKE SURE NOTHING STICKS IN YOUR THROAT.

All gone!

CUT PILLS MAY TASTE NASTY. SIP A LITTLE WATER, TIP YOUR HEAD BACK, HOLD THE WATER IN THE BACK OF YOUR MOUTH, DROP THE PILL DIRECTLY INTO THE WATER, & SWALLOW AS ABOVE WITH PLENTY MORE WATER. HAVE A FLAVORFUL CHASER READY.

⭐ AROUND & ABOUT

● A **PILLBOX** IS USEFUL FOR KEEPING SOME MEDS WITH YOU, IN SOMETHING PROTECTIVE, EASILY FINDABLE, & PERHAPS PRETTY, & NOT CRUMBLING IN THE LINTY LINING OF YOUR BAG.

COTTON, SO THE PILLS DON'T RATTLE OR CRUMBLE

A PILLBOX IS ALSO USEFUL IF YOU EVER SLEEP AWAY FROM HOME UNEXPECTEDLY. KEEP A COUPLE DOSES OF YOUR REGULAR MEDS WITH YOU, & YOU CAN BE FLEXIBLE LIKE THAT.

PRN ("AS NEEDED")

SET OF AM & PM MEDS

MAYBE IBUPROFEN OR SOMETHING FOR GAS OR WHATEVER

MAKE SURE YOU CAN IDENTIFY YOUR PILLS!!

GIVE YOURSELF A

● **TREAT** AFTER ANY PART OF TREATMENT THAT YOU FIND A REAL PAIN. FOR ME THAT'S BLOOD DRAWS.

THIS REALLY WORKS!

MAKE YOUR TREAT:

☆ CONVENIENT, SO YOU CAN DO IT IMMEDIATELY AFTERWARDS

☆ SPECIAL(ISH), SOMETHING YOU WOULDN'T NORMALLY DO OR GET.

what is your lollipop?

MINE TEND TO BE OVERPRICED BEVERAGES.

ICED MATCHA MINT MATE SOY LATTE

STRAWBERRY MILK

organic moo

RASPBERRY KOMBUCHA

with chia

☆ TRAVEL

- HAVE MEDS ON YOUR
PACKING CHECKLIST
FORGOT YOUR TOOTHBRUSH? YOU CAN
GET THOSE ANYWHERE. FORGOT YOUR
MEDS? MUCH MORE OF A PAIN.

- SURPRISINGLY VAGUE **TSA RULES:**
"IT IS RECOMMENDED THAT MEDICATION BE CLEARLY LABELED."
FOR INTERNATIONAL TRAVEL, KEEP YOUR MEDS IN THEIR
ORIGINAL BOTTLES.

IT'S A GOOD IDEA TO KEEP MEDS IN THEIR BOTTLES.
BUT IF YOU DON'T WANT TO LUG ALL THAT AROUND,

- PUT THEM IN
SOMETHING CONVENIENT

I FOUND THAT PUTTING THEM IN A
REGULAR PILL BOTTLE MEANT I COULDN'T
REACH IN FOR THE RIGHT KIND & NUMBER...

SO I'D HAVE TO DUMP
THEM OUT INTO MY
HAND OR SOMEWHERE.

gah

yikes!

Don't
sneeze!

I SUGGEST A

REPURPOSED CONTAINER THAT SEALS WELL
(WATERTIGHT IS GREAT), OPENS EASILY SO YOU DON'T SPILL
EVERYTHING TRYING TO GET IT OPEN, & IS RELATIVELY FLAT
SO THE PILLS ARE EASY TO POKE THROUGH.

NOT
MANY
PILLS

QUITE
A FEW
PILLS

MED ZEPPELIN

SMALL PERSONAL
CARE PRODUCT
JARS ARE GREAT.

OPTIONAL: PEEL OFF THE LABEL;
SCRUB IT OFF WITH STEEL
WOOL; PUT A STICKER ON IT.

STUFF THE EXTRA
SPACE WITH COTTON
BALLS SO THE PILLS
DON'T RATTLE OR
CRUMBLE.

KEEP YOUR MEDS WITH YOU

ON YOUR PERSON OR IN YOUR CARRY-ON, IN CASE YOUR TRANSPORT IS RIDICULOUSLY DELAYED OR YOUR BAG IS LOST OR STOLEN.

IF YOUR GENERICS ARE IN THE SAME CONTAINER, MAKE SURE YOU CAN TELL THEM APART!

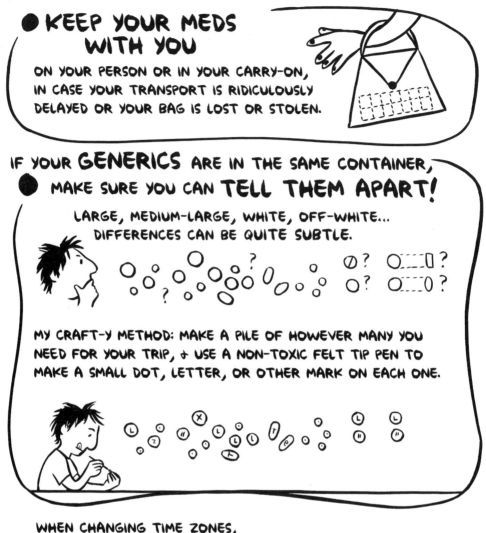

LARGE, MEDIUM-LARGE, WHITE, OFF-WHITE... DIFFERENCES CAN BE QUITE SUBTLE.

MY CRAFT-Y METHOD: MAKE A PILE OF HOWEVER MANY YOU NEED FOR YOUR TRIP, & USE A NON-TOXIC FELT TIP PEN TO MAKE A SMALL DOT, LETTER, OR OTHER MARK ON EACH ONE.

WHEN CHANGING TIME ZONES,

KEEP YOUR REGULAR MED SCHEDULE

AS MUCH AS POSSIBLE.

MATCH YOUR MED SCHEDULE WITH YOUR SLEEP SCHEDULE, TRANSITIONING ASAP TO YOUR NEW TIME ZONE.

OR POSSIBLY, FOR SHORT TRIPS, STICK TO YOUR HOME TIME ZONE SCHEDULE FOR EVERYTHING.

BRING A COUPLE DAYS' EXTRA

PERHAPS YOU WILL STAY A LITTLE LONGER.
PERHAPS SOME DROP & ROLL INTO A VENT.

RAN OUT? MISCOUNTED?
IT'S NOT THAT HARD TO

GET MORE ON THE ROAD.

IF YOU CAN, FIND OUT IF YOUR INSURANCE WILL COVER
THEM. IF NOT, JUST GET ENOUGH FOR A FEW DAYS.

FIND THE NUMBER OF A
PHARMACY NEARBY.

CALL YOUR DOCTOR WITH
THEIR NUMBER.

BRING YOUR INSURANCE CARD,
IF NECESSARY.

IF YOU CAN'T REACH
YOUR DOCTOR,
YOU CAN ASK THE
PHARMACY IF THEY'LL
TRANSFER YOUR
PRESCRIPTION & GIVE
YOU A SMALL SUPPLY.

⭐ SIDE EFFECTS

STARTING A NEW MED? **LOOK IT UP,** & **DON'T FREAK OUT** AT THE LONG LIST OF SIDE EFFECTS!

YOU DEFINITELY NEED TO **WATCH OUT** FOR THEM, BUT THE WEIRD ONES PROBABLY WON'T HAPPEN TO YOU.

BE SURE TO **TELL YOUR DOCTOR** IF YOU'RE HAVING SIDE EFFECTS – YOUR MEDS MAY NEED TO BE CHANGED OR ADJUSTED.

It might make me pee rainbows!!

IN THE MEANTIME, HERE ARE SOME THINGS YOU MIGHT TRY FOR SOME OF THE MOST **COMMON** ONES.

FOR MEMORY PROBLEMS

☆ KEEP THINGS IN ONE REGULAR PLACE

☆ SET AN ALARM

☆ LEAVE YOURSELF A REMINDER THAT YOU WILL SEE AT THE RIGHT TIME. *get bananas*

FOR WEIGHT GAIN

☆ TRACK YOUR EATING

☆ EXERCISE

☆ THINK "HEALTHY" INSTEAD OF "THIN"

☆ LOOK UP "PLUS-SIZE" MODELS

☆ FOCUS ON ACCEPTING & LOVING YOUR BODY!!

☆ READ ACTOR WENTWORTH MILLER'S POSTS ON SURVIVING SUICIDAL THOUGHTS & TAKING ANTIDEPRESSANTS. *I gained weight. Big f--ing deal.*

FOR SEXUAL PROBLEMS

☆ GET YOURSELF STARTED PHYSICALLY, & MAYBE YOUR MIND WILL FOLLOW.

☆ IT MIGHT STILL BE FUN TO PLEASURE YOUR PARTNER.

☆ VIAGRA

☆ TOYS, PORN, ANYTHING THAT NORMALLY TURNS YOU ON

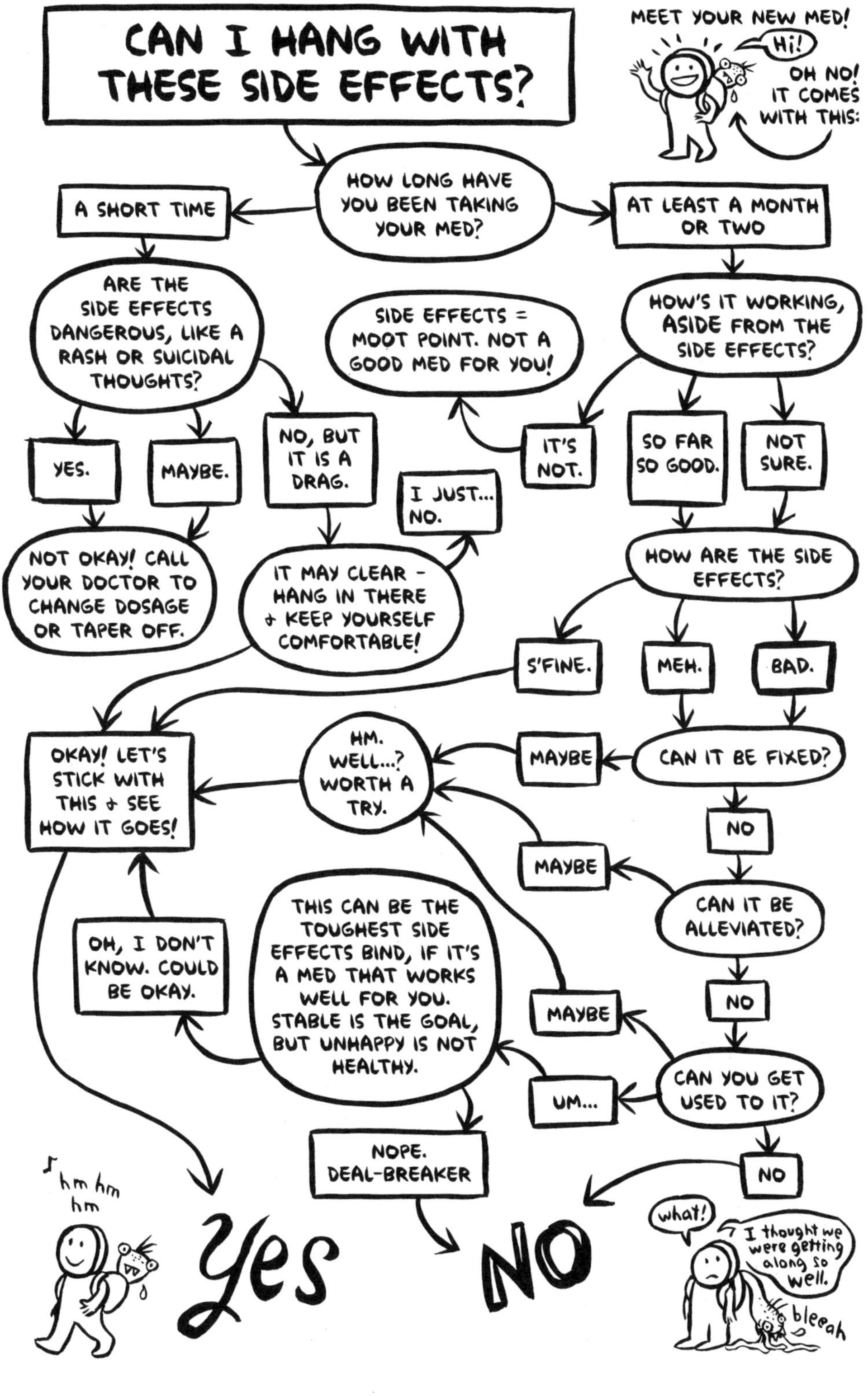
CAN I HANG WITH THESE SIDE EFFECTS?
MEET YOUR NEW MED!
Hi!
OH NO! IT COMES WITH THIS:
HOW LONG HAVE YOU BEEN TAKING YOUR MED?
A SHORT TIME
AT LEAST A MONTH OR TWO
ARE THE SIDE EFFECTS DANGEROUS, LIKE A RASH OR SUICIDAL THOUGHTS?
SIDE EFFECTS = MOOT POINT. NOT A GOOD MED FOR YOU!
HOW'S IT WORKING, ASIDE FROM THE SIDE EFFECTS?
YES.
MAYBE.
NO, BUT IT IS A DRAG.
IT'S NOT.
SO FAR SO GOOD.
NOT SURE.
I JUST... NO.
NOT OKAY! CALL YOUR DOCTOR TO CHANGE DOSAGE OR TAPER OFF.
IT MAY CLEAR - HANG IN THERE & KEEP YOURSELF COMFORTABLE!
HOW ARE THE SIDE EFFECTS?
S'FINE.
MEH.
BAD.
OKAY! LET'S STICK WITH THIS & SEE HOW IT GOES!
HM. WELL...? WORTH A TRY.
MAYBE
CAN IT BE FIXED?
NO
MAYBE
CAN IT BE ALLEVIATED?
OH, I DON'T KNOW. COULD BE OKAY.
THIS CAN BE THE TOUGHEST SIDE EFFECTS BIND, IF IT'S A MED THAT WORKS WELL FOR YOU. STABLE IS THE GOAL, BUT UNHAPPY IS NOT HEALTHY.
NO
MAYBE
UM...
CAN YOU GET USED TO IT?
NOPE. DEAL-BREAKER
NO
hm hm hm
YES
NO
what!
I thought we were getting along so well.
bleeah

MERIT BADGES FOR
MEDS

STAYING THE
COURSE

PLACE TO
KEEP 'EM

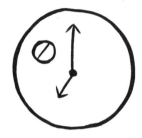

REMEMBERING
TO TAKE 'EM

PILL-CUTTING

SWALLOW IN
ONE GULP

TREAT!

CRAFTY TRAVEL
CONTAINER

ON THE ROAD

SIDE EFFECTS

CHAPTER 6
THE
DANGER ZONE

YOU CAN USE YOUR COPING TOOLS ANYTIME, MIXING &
MATCHING & CREATING NEW ONES. BUT AN ESSENTIAL PART
OF ROCKING STEADY IS TO HAVE YOUR TOOLBOX AT THE
READY WHEN YOU MIGHT BE FACING DOWN AN EPISODE.

WE NEED TO BE ABLE TO PREDICT, RECOGNIZE, & PREVENT
OR STOP AN EPISODE WHILE THERE'S STILL TIME TO CHECK ALL
THE GAUGES, MAKE A PLAN, TAKE THOSE STEPS, &/OR GET HELP.

THERE ARE A COUPLE OF DANGER ZONES LEVELS TO BE AWARE OF.

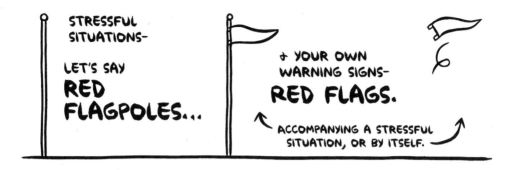

STRESSFUL SITUATIONS-

LET'S SAY **RED FLAGPOLES...**

& YOUR OWN WARNING SIGNS-
RED FLAGS.

← ACCOMPANYING A STRESSFUL SITUATION, OR BY ITSELF. →

RED FLAGPOLES ARE THINGS GOING ON IN YOUR LIFE OR IN THE WORLD THAT MIGHT KNOCK YOU OFF BALANCE.

RED FLAGS ARE BASICALLY BABY SYMPTOMS. WE WANT TO CATCH THESE BEFORE THEY TURN INTO FULL-ON SYMPTOMS OF A FULL-ON EPISODE. SO THEY MAY NOT BE A PROBLEM YET, WHICH IS EXACTLY WHY THEY'RE HARD TO RECOGNIZE OR PRIORITIZE.

DANGER ZONE LEVEL #1:
RED FLAGPOLES

RED FLAGPOLES MIGHT OR MIGHT NOT LEAD TO TROUBLE. BUT IF YOU'RE IN A STRESSFUL SITUATION OR IF THERE'S ONE ON THE HORIZON, OR ESPECIALLY IF THEY START TO PILE UP, IT'S TIME TO BE EXTRA AWARE OF YOUR MOODS & BEHAVIOR.

CHANGE OF SEASONS

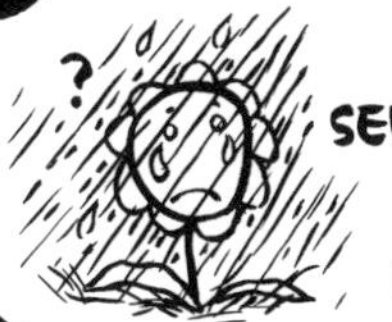
?

PEOPLE WITH MOOD DISORDERS SEEM ESPECIALLY SENSITIVE TO THIS.

THE MOOD CHANGES MAY NOT BE INTUITIVE! I'M MORE LIKELY TO BE UP IN THE WINTER & DOWN IN THE SUMMER.

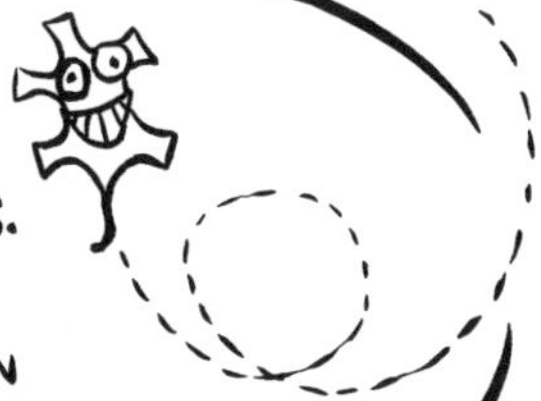

ANYTHING STRESSFUL IN YOUR LIFE, BAD OR GOOD

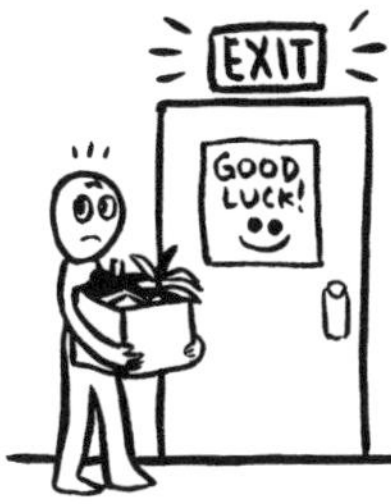
EXIT
GOOD LUCK!

LOSS OF JOB

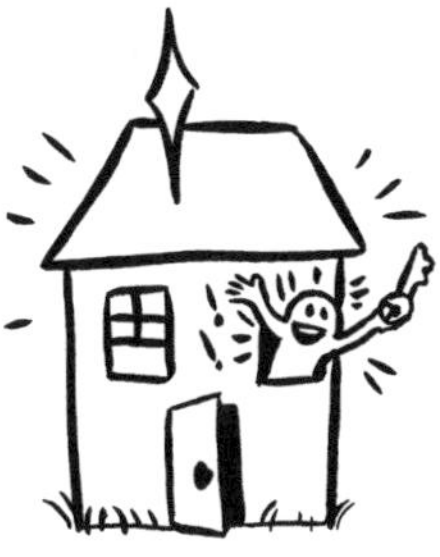

NEW HOUSE

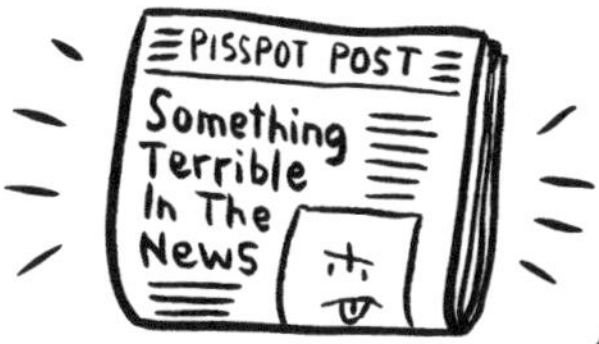
PISSPOT POST
Something Terrible In The News

GRIEF SOMEONE CLOSE, OR EVEN NOT SO CLOSE.

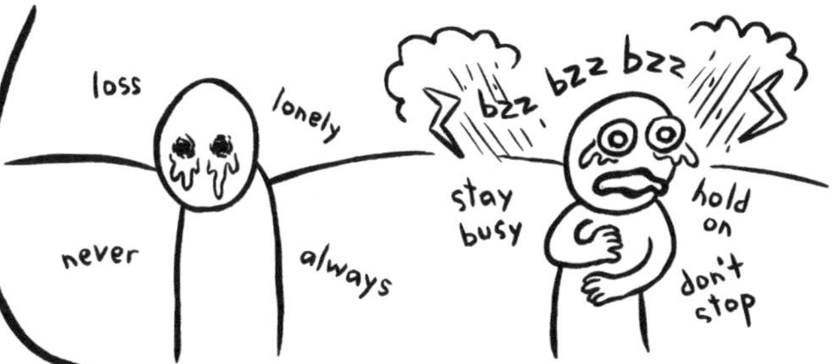
loss
lonely
never
always
bzz bzz bzz
stay busy
hold on
don't stop

IT MAY SEEM INTUITIVE THAT GRIEF COULD LEAD TO DEPRESSION, BUT A MIND & BODY IN OVERDRIVE COULD TRIGGER A MANIC EPISODE, TOO.

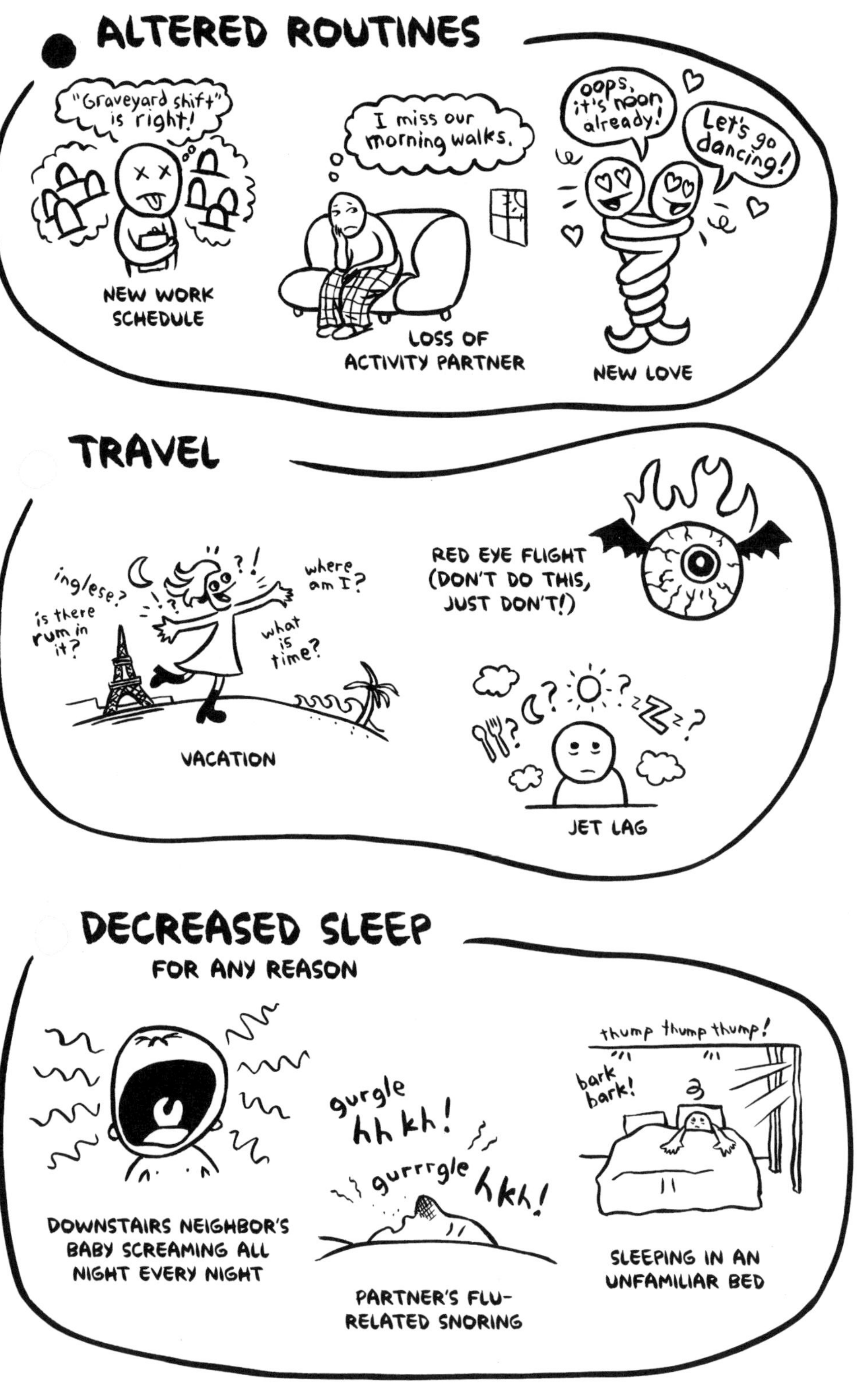
ALTERED ROUTINES
"Graveyard shift" is right!
NEW WORK SCHEDULE
I miss our morning walks.
LOSS OF ACTIVITY PARTNER
oops, it's noon already!
Let's go dancing!
NEW LOVE
TRAVEL
inglese?
is there rum in it?
?!
where am I?
what is time?
VACATION
RED EYE FLIGHT (DON'T DO THIS, JUST DON'T!)
JET LAG
DECREASED SLEEP
FOR ANY REASON
DOWNSTAIRS NEIGHBOR'S BABY SCREAMING ALL NIGHT EVERY NIGHT
gurgle hhkh!
gurrrgle hkh!
PARTNER'S FLU-RELATED SNORING
thump thump thump!
bark bark!
SLEEPING IN AN UNFAMILIAR BED

TREATMENT-RELATED THINGS

CHANGES IN MEDS

Again?!
crap!

FORGETTING TO TAKE YOUR MEDS

REGULAR DOCTOR IS ON VACATION

ISOLATION

It's so quiet
quiet
quiet
quiet
P.j.'s

WORKING FROM HOME

I've been talking to myself all day...
I miss you!!
Hi!
OMG Hi!

PARTNER IS AWAY

ILLNESS OR INJURY

LIMITED MOVEMENT

!?

NEW AFFLICTION
NEW HEALTH NEEDS
NEW UNKNOWNS

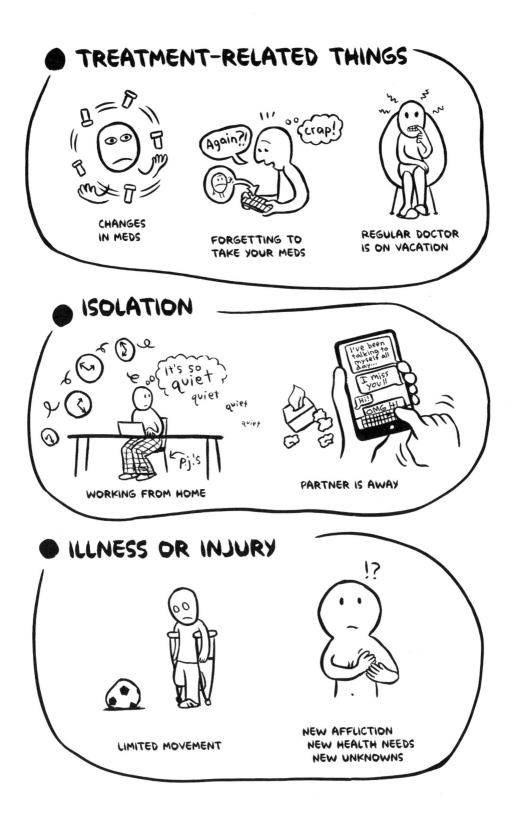

DANGER ZONE LEVEL #2:
RED FLAGS

RED FLAGS ARE YOUR WARNING SIGNS THAT YOU MAY HAVE AN EPISODE BREWING. THEY'RE A BIT DIFFERENT FOR EVERYONE (BUT ALMOST ALWAYS INCLUDE DISRUPTED SLEEP). TO LEARN WHAT YOUR RED FLAGS ARE & NOTICE WHEN THEY'RE APPEARING, IT HELPS TO KNOW THE PATTERNS OF YOUR OWN STABLE NORMAL ("EUTHYMIA").

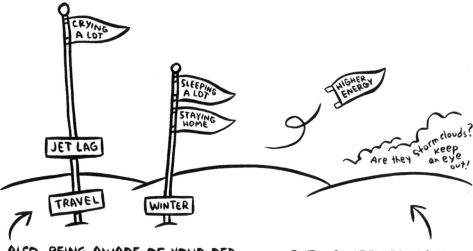

ALSO, BEING AWARE OF YOUR RED FLAGPOLES WILL MAKE IT EASIER TO KNOW WHEN TO BE EXTRA ON THE LOOKOUT FOR RED FLAGS.*

THE RED FLAGS THAT FOLLOW ARE DIVIDED INTO COMMON DANGER SIGNS FOR MANIA & DEPRESSION, BUT THEY'RE NOT NECESSARILY SO DISTINCT.

BUT... SOMETIMES FLAGS COME UP JUST BECAUSE MOOD DISORDER.

FOR EXAMPLE, INCREASED ANXIOUS ENERGY COULD BE A RED FLAG FOR MANIA OR DEPRESSION, DEPENDING ON YOUR OWN PATTERNS.

*RED FLAGS THAT STEM FROM A PARTICULAR TRAUMATIC SITUATION *MIGHT* INDICATE SITUATIONAL DEPRESSION INSTEAD OF MAJOR OR BIPOLAR DEPRESSION. BE SURE TO GET AN ACCURATE DIAGNOSIS, & MAKE SURE YOUR DOCTOR IS AWARE OF YOUR RED FLAGPOLES!

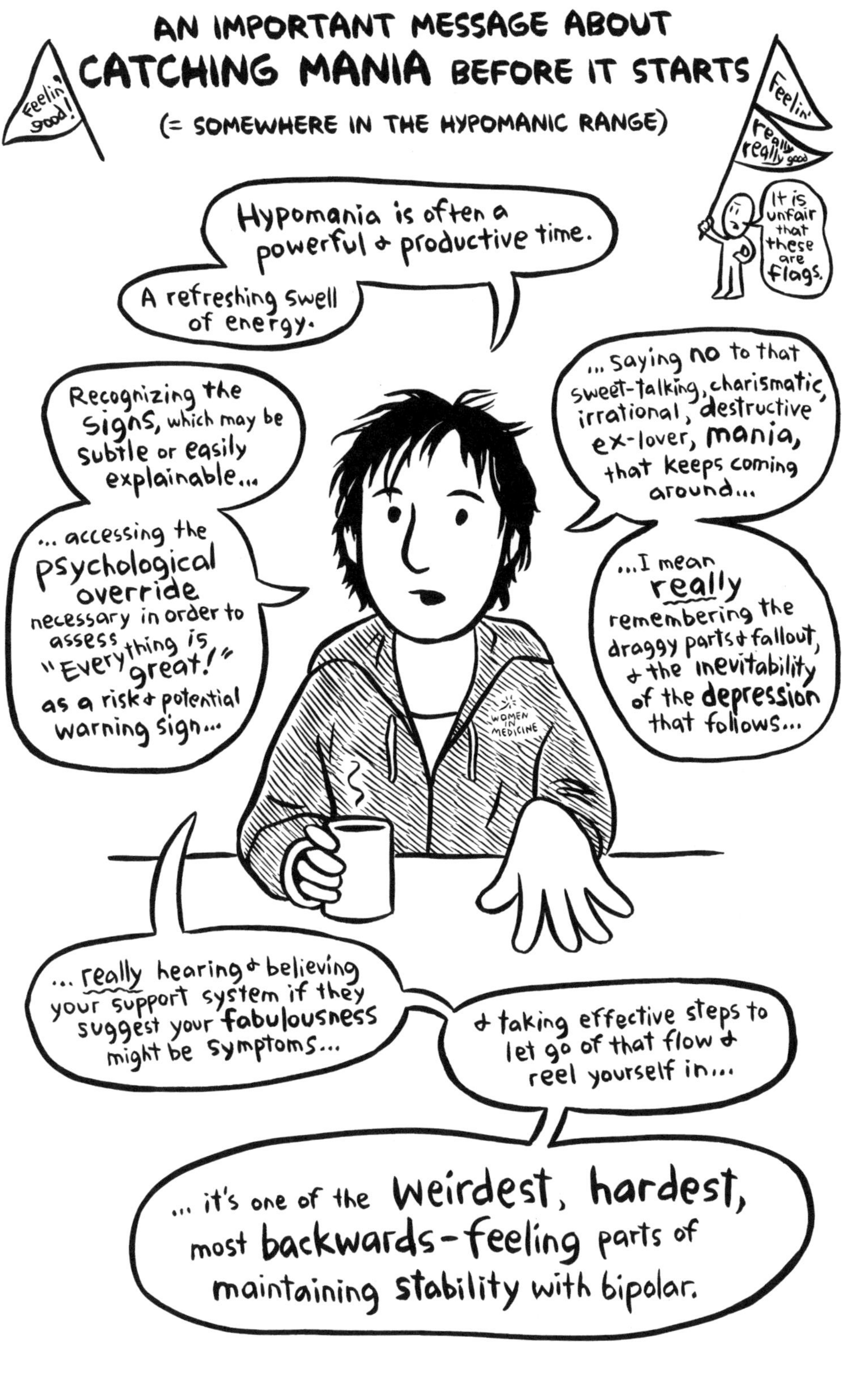
AN IMPORTANT MESSAGE ABOUT
CATCHING MANIA BEFORE IT STARTS
(= SOMEWHERE IN THE HYPOMANIC RANGE)
Feelin' good!
Feelin' really really really good
It is unfair that these are flags.
Hypomania is often a powerful & productive time.
A refreshing swell of energy.
Recognizing the signs, which may be subtle or easily explainable...
... accessing the psychological override necessary in order to assess "Everything is great!" as a risk & potential warning sign...
... saying no to that sweet-talking, charismatic, irrational, destructive ex-lover, mania, that keeps coming around...
... I mean really remembering the draggy parts & fallout, & the inevitability of the depression that follows...
WOMEN IN MEDICINE
... really hearing & believing your support system if they suggest your fabulousness might be symptoms...
& taking effective steps to let go of that flow & reel yourself in...
... it's one of the weirdest, hardest, most backwards-feeling parts of maintaining stability with bipolar.

RED FLAGS FOR MANIA INCLUDE:

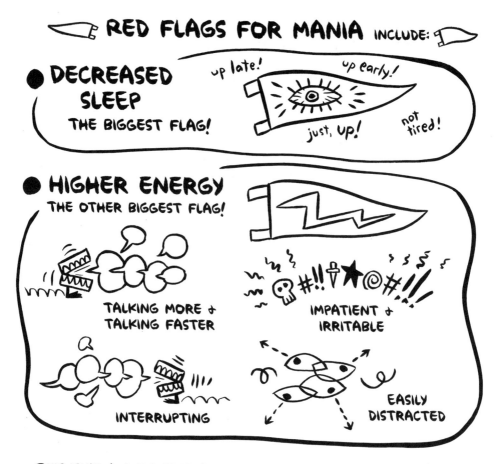

- **DECREASED SLEEP**
  THE BIGGEST FLAG!

  up late! up early! just, up! not tired!

- **HIGHER ENERGY**
  THE OTHER BIGGEST FLAG!

  TALKING MORE & TALKING FASTER

  IMPATIENT & IRRITABLE

  INTERRUPTING

  EASILY DISTRACTED

THIS ISN'T A JUDGMENT ABOUT THE APPROPRIATENESS OR INAPPROPRIATENESS OF GOING OUT DANCING EVERY NIGHT. IT'S MORE LIKE,

- IS IT UNUSUAL FOR YOU?
- IS IT KEEPING YOU FROM GETTING YOUR REGULAR STUFF DONE?
- DOES IT SEEM LIKE YOUR FRIENDS CAN'T KEEP UP?

- ARE YOU FEELING SUPER ON TOP OF EVERYTHING EVEN THOUGH THINGS HAVEN'T CHANGED?

toing! boing! boing! bownng! bwoing! doing!

THIS MAY BE YOUR NORMAL.

HERE IS YOUR RED FLAG! DO YOUR SELF-CARE RED FLAG THINGS!

DAH! TOO LATE. TIME TO DEAL WITH **MANIA.**

LOWER APPETITE LESS EATING

lonely banana

● SPENDING MONEY MORE EASILY

come play

IMPULSE BUYS MORE TEMPTING

INCREASED SPENDING ON CREDIT CARDS

CASINO SPREE

MAKING BIG PLANS

BIG IDEAS ARE IMPORTANT. BUT IF YOUR IDEA FEELS MIND-BLOWINGLY IMPORTANT & LIKE IT CAN'T WAIT, YOU MIGHT CONSIDER IF IT'S A RED FLAG.

We'll call our company International Bake Sale!

Cricket muffins could solve world hunger!

● MORE SEXY GOING ON

FLIRTING MORE THAN USUAL

CONSIDERING AN AFFAIR

THINKING ABOUT OR HAVING WAY MORE SEX THAN USUAL

AT LEAST BE SAFE, BUT MAYBE YOU CAN JUST DO YOURSELF A LOT FOR NOW.

Everything is about Sex

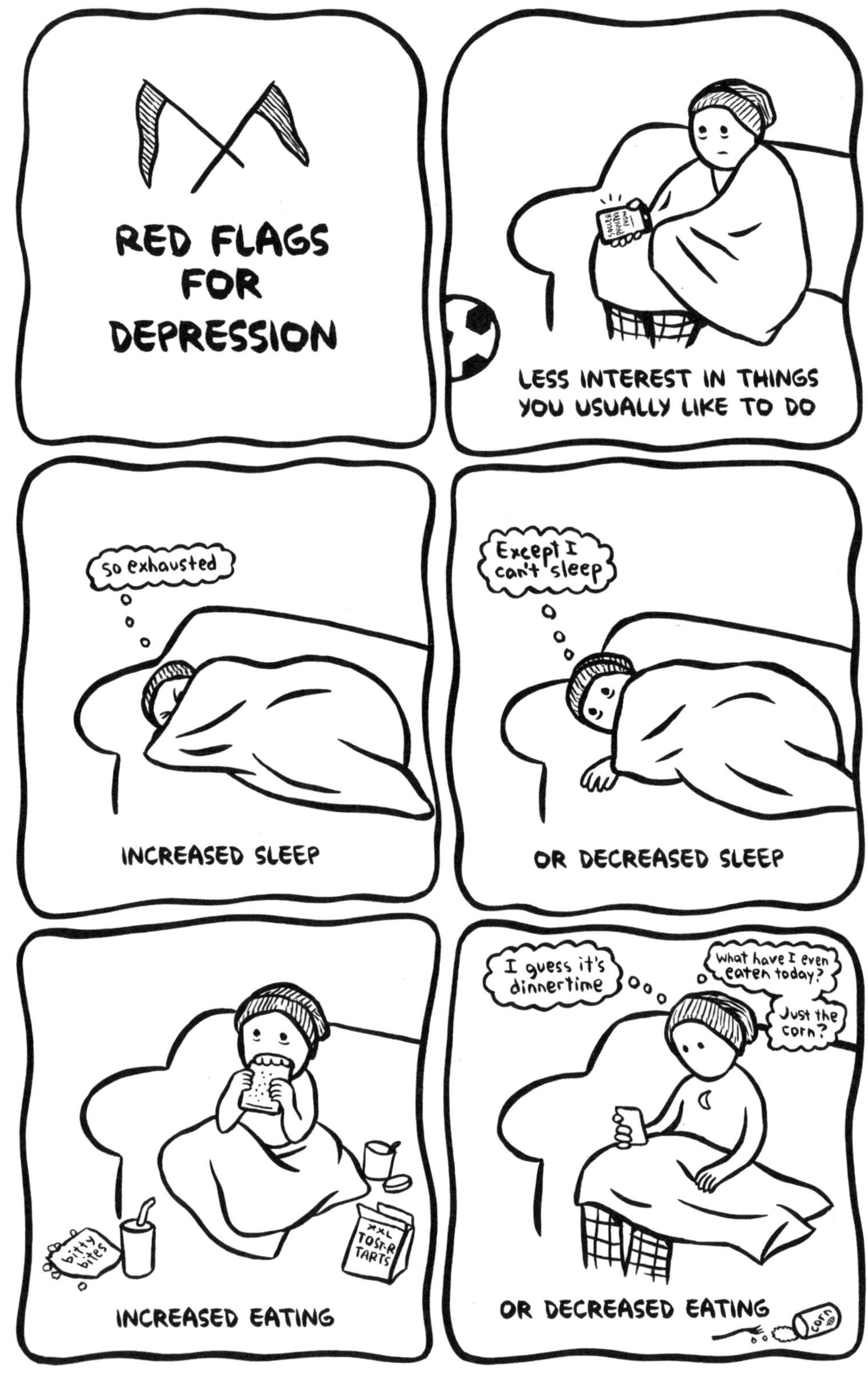
RED FLAGS FOR DEPRESSION
LESS INTEREST IN THINGS YOU USUALLY LIKE TO DO
so exhausted
INCREASED SLEEP
Except I can't sleep
OR DECREASED SLEEP
bitty bites
XXL TOST-R TARTS
INCREASED EATING
I guess it's dinnertime
What have I even eaten today?
Just the corn?
OR DECREASED EATING
corn

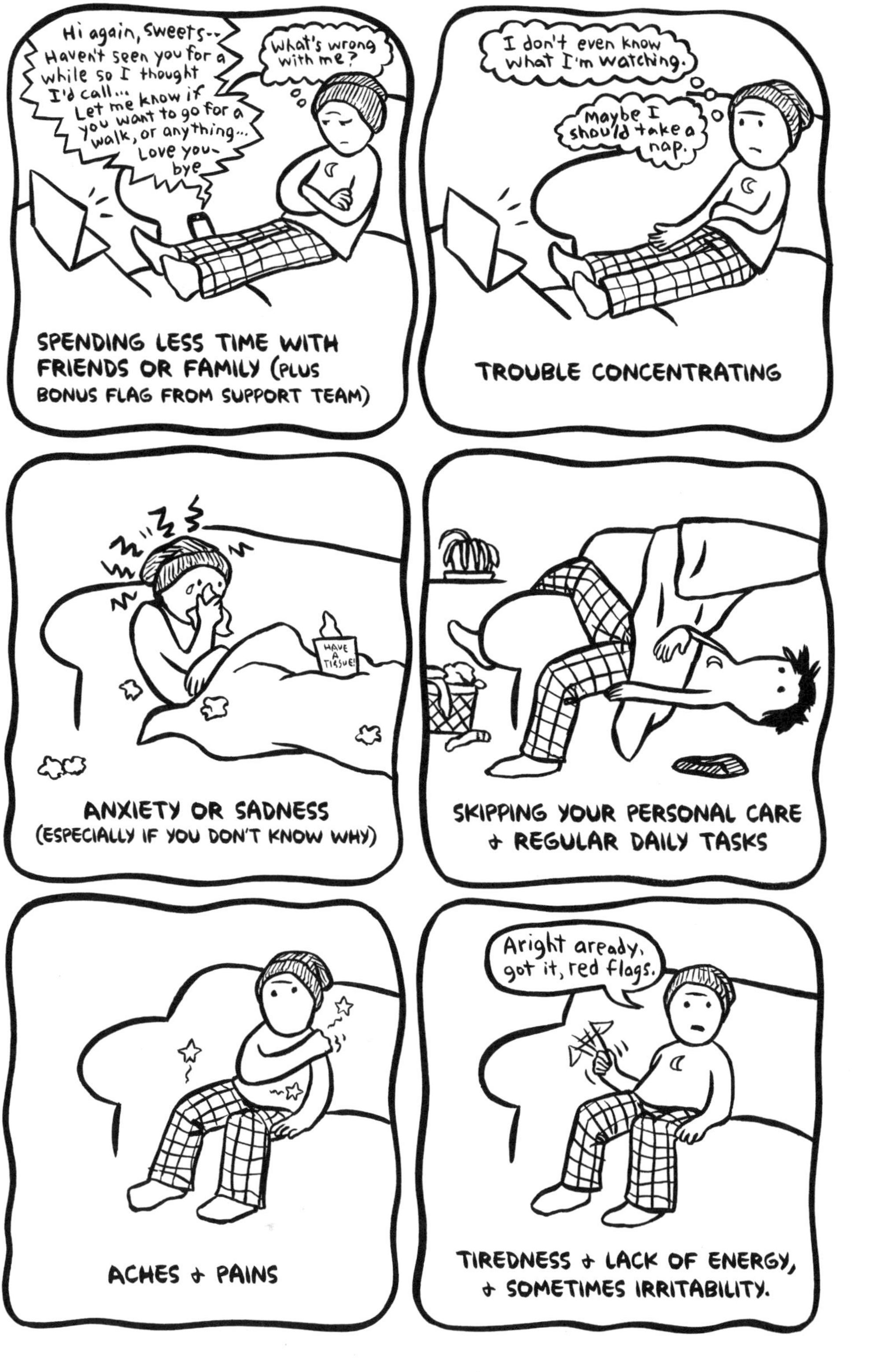
Hi again, sweets-- Haven't seen you for a while so I thought I'd call... Let me know if you want to go for a walk, or anything... Love you- bye
What's wrong with me?
SPENDING LESS TIME WITH FRIENDS OR FAMILY (PLUS BONUS FLAG FROM SUPPORT TEAM)
I don't even know what I'm watching.
Maybe I should take a nap.
TROUBLE CONCENTRATING
HAVE A TISSUE!
ANXIETY OR SADNESS (ESPECIALLY IF YOU DON'T KNOW WHY)
SKIPPING YOUR PERSONAL CARE + REGULAR DAILY TASKS
ACHES + PAINS
Aright aready, got it, red flags.
TIREDNESS + LACK OF ENERGY, + SOMETIMES IRRITABILITY.

RED FLAGS
FOR MANIA OR DEPRESSION OR OTHER DISORDERLY TUMBLE OF MOODS

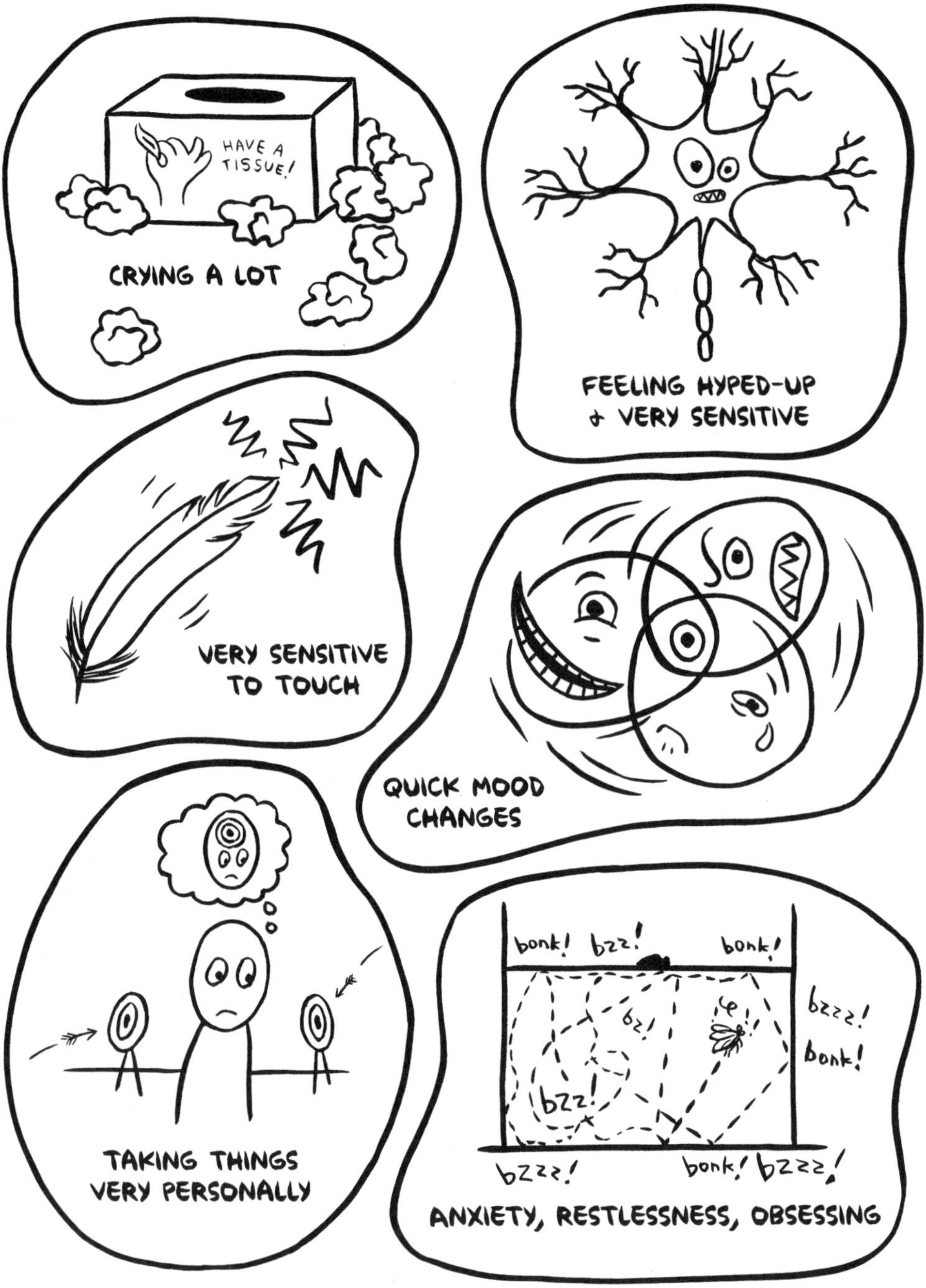
HAVE A TISSUE!
CRYING A LOT
FEELING HYPED-UP & VERY SENSITIVE
VERY SENSITIVE TO TOUCH
QUICK MOOD CHANGES
TAKING THINGS VERY PERSONALLY
bonk! bzz! bonk!
bzzz! bonk!
bz!
bzz!
bzzz! bonk! bzzz!
ANXIETY, RESTLESSNESS, OBSESSING

⭐ IDENTIFY **YOUR** DANGER ZONES

WHAT ARE YOUR
RED FLAGPOLES?

TRAVELING?

DATING
SOMEONE
NEW?

NEW
SEMESTER?

GETTING TOGETHER
WITH YOUR FAMILY?

SUMMER?

WHAT ARE YOUR
RED FLAGS?

TROUBLE
SLEEPING?

CRYING BUT
YOU DON'T
KNOW WHY?

INTERRUPTING
PEOPLE?

IF YOU DON'T GET
ENOUGH SLEEP, DOES
THAT MAKE YOU
TIRED? OR SPEEDY?

THESE ARE MY
OWN BIGGEST
FLAGS.

LOOK BACK.

WHEN DID YOUR SYMPTOMS START?
WHAT HAPPENED?

IT CAN BE FRUSTRATING TO PEER INTO THE PAST FOR WHAT YOUR ALERTS MAY HAVE BEEN. WHAT? WHEN? FOR HOW LONG? ESPECIALLY SINCE THEY MAY HAVE SEEMED INNOCUOUS OR EXPLAINABLE AT THE TIME.

● A **JOURNAL** IS GREAT FOR THIS KIND OF SLEUTHING.

MAY–JUNE

● A **MOOD CHART** CAN HELP YOU SEE PATTERNS & CORRELATIONS, ESPECIALLY IF YOU'RE ALSO JOURNALING.

(MORE ON CHARTS IN A FEW PAGES.)

● A **PERCEPTIVE DOCTOR** IS AWESOME.

Hm... you started revving last winter, too.

Hm!

LISTEN TO THE PEOPLE YOU TRUST

Move to China?

Did you actually put crickets in those muffins?

Heyyy...those are some big plans all of a sudden. You said you just started new meds, right? Do you think you might be getting a bit manic?

ting!

Hiii

You've seemed kind of low, are you okay?

THIS CAN BE DIFFICULT TO FINESSE, FOR EVERYONE INVOLVED. CLEAR COMMUNICATION & BOUNDARIES ARE REALLY IMPORTANT!

LET'S SAY YOU'VE DETECTED SOME RED FLAGS.

OKAY. EXCELLENT INSIGHT!

NOW WHAT?

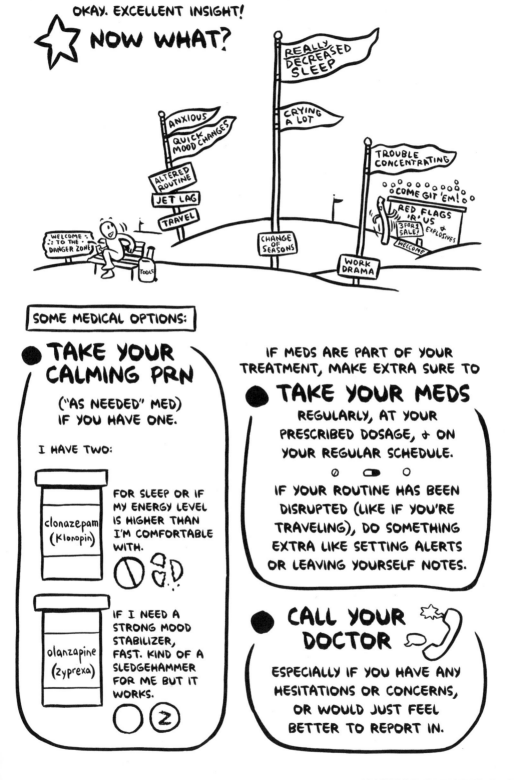

REALLY DECREASED SLEEP

CRYING A LOT

ANXIOUS

QUICK MOOD CHANGES

ALTERED ROUTINE

JET LAG

TRAVEL

TROUBLE CONCENTRATING

COME GIT 'EM!

RED FLAGS 'R' US & EXPLOSIVES

3 FOR 1 SALE!

WELCOME

WELCOME TO THE DANGER ZONE

TOOLS

CHANGE OF SEASONS

WORK DRAMA

SOME MEDICAL OPTIONS:

• TAKE YOUR CALMING PRN

("AS NEEDED" MED) IF YOU HAVE ONE.

I HAVE TWO:

clonazepam (Klonopin)

FOR SLEEP OR IF MY ENERGY LEVEL IS HIGHER THAN I'M COMFORTABLE WITH.

olanzapine (Zyprexa)

IF I NEED A STRONG MOOD STABILIZER, FAST. KIND OF A SLEDGEHAMMER FOR ME BUT IT WORKS.

Ⓩ

IF MEDS ARE PART OF YOUR TREATMENT, MAKE EXTRA SURE TO

• TAKE YOUR MEDS

REGULARLY, AT YOUR PRESCRIBED DOSAGE, & ON YOUR REGULAR SCHEDULE.

IF YOUR ROUTINE HAS BEEN DISRUPTED (LIKE IF YOU'RE TRAVELING), DO SOMETHING EXTRA LIKE SETTING ALERTS OR LEAVING YOURSELF NOTES.

• CALL YOUR DOCTOR

ESPECIALLY IF YOU HAVE ANY HESITATIONS OR CONCERNS, OR WOULD JUST FEEL BETTER TO REPORT IN.

TOOLS IN PREVIOUS CHAPTERS COULD BE ESPECIALLY USEFUL RIGHT NOW. CONCENTRATE ON YOUR FAVORITES OR TRY SOMETHING NEW.

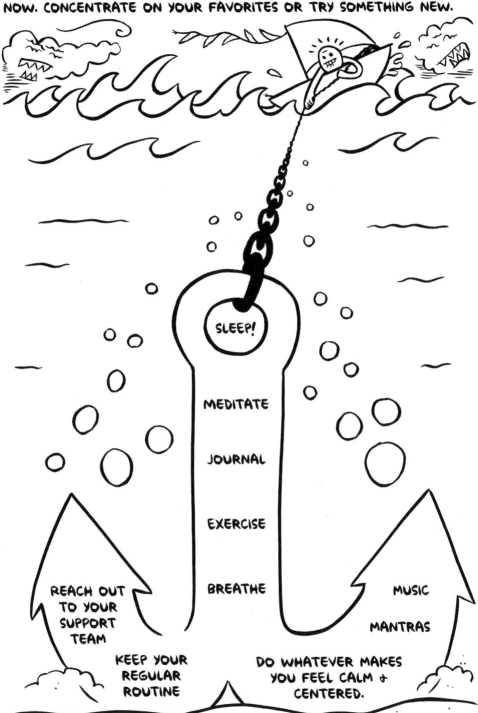

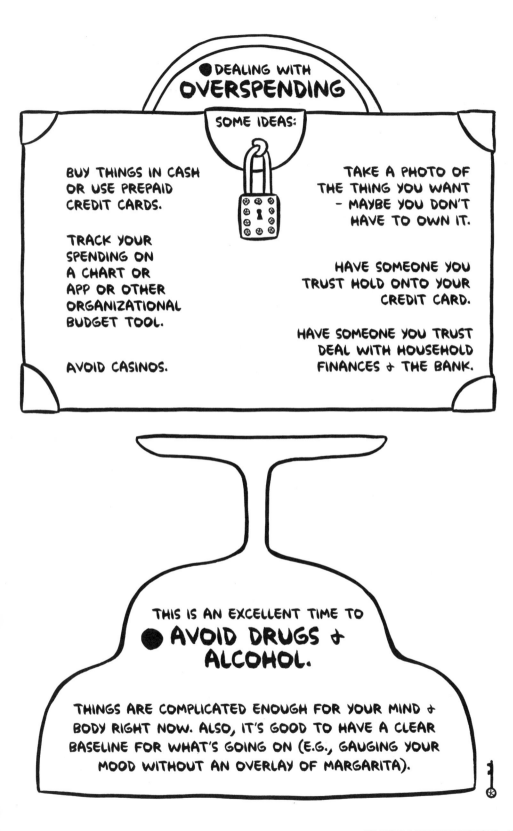

● DEALING WITH OVERSPENDING

SOME IDEAS:

BUY THINGS IN CASH OR USE PREPAID CREDIT CARDS.

TRACK YOUR SPENDING ON A CHART OR APP OR OTHER ORGANIZATIONAL BUDGET TOOL.

AVOID CASINOS.

TAKE A PHOTO OF THE THING YOU WANT – MAYBE YOU DON'T HAVE TO OWN IT.

HAVE SOMEONE YOU TRUST HOLD ONTO YOUR CREDIT CARD.

HAVE SOMEONE YOU TRUST DEAL WITH HOUSEHOLD FINANCES & THE BANK.

THIS IS AN EXCELLENT TIME TO

● AVOID DRUGS & ALCOHOL.

THINGS ARE COMPLICATED ENOUGH FOR YOUR MIND & BODY RIGHT NOW. ALSO, IT'S GOOD TO HAVE A CLEAR BASELINE FOR WHAT'S GOING ON (E.G., GAUGING YOUR MOOD WITHOUT AN OVERLAY OF MARGARITA).

● KEEP TRACK.

TRACKING IS ALWAYS HELPFUL AS PART OF YOUR ROUTINE SELF-CARE, BUT IF IT'S NOT SOMETHING YOU DO REGULARLY, NOW IS THE TIME TO MAKE AN EXTRA EFFORT.

TRACKING YOUR MOOD & ACTIVITIES WILL HELP YOU:

☆ KEEP THINGS IN CHECK NOW,

☆ DETERMINE FLAGS & FLAGPOLES WHEN YOU LOOK BACK LATER,

☆ TELL YOUR DOCTOR WHAT YOU'RE GOING THROUGH, WITHOUT YOUR NEEDING TO TRY TO RECONSTRUCT EVERYTHING BY MEMORY AT YOUR NEXT APPOINTMENT, SO THEY CAN HELP YOU FIGURE OUT YOUR PATTERNS.

YOU CAN TRY:

● MOOD TRACKING APPS

THERE ARE MANY, OF COURSE. SOME SEND THE INFORMATION DIRECTLY TO YOUR DOCTOR, SOME CORRESPOND WITH OTHER PEOPLE, & THERE ARE MANY FANCY ONES IN DEVELOPMENT.

YOU COULD LOOK AROUND PSYBERGUIDE.ORG, A CONSUMER GUIDE FOR MENTAL HEALTH APPS & GADGETRY. (these are not real!)

Me'N'My Moods | Track & Snack | Moody Moody Mood Mood | Up & Down Burger

DOWNLOADABLE THERAPY-SPECIFIC
● MOOD CHART TEMPLATES

MANY ORGANIZATIONS OFFER THESE FREE ON THEIR WEBSITES.

SAMPLE IPSRT CHART ON THE NEXT PAGE ⟩

YOUR OWN
● CUSTOM CHART

ALLOWS MORE FLEXIBILITY, EVEN DRAWINGS & PROSE

MY METHOD ON THE PAGE AFTER THAT ⟩

SOME MOOD CHARTS ARE VERY STRUCTURED & SPECIFIC TO A PARTICULAR THERAPY. THIS IS AN EXAMPLE OF A WORKSHEET IN INTERPERSONAL & SOCIAL RHYTHM THERAPY (IPSRT), WHICH HAS A FOCUS ON KEEPING TO A ROUTINE.

Social Rhythm Metric-II- Five-Item Version (SRM II –5)

Date (week of): _____

Directions:
Write the ideal target time you would like to do these daily activities.
Record the time you actually did the activity each day.
Record the people involved in the activity: 0 = Alone; 1 = Others present; 2 = Others actively involved; 3 = Others very stimulating

Activity	Target Time	Sunday		Monday		Tuesday		Wednesday		Thursday		Friday		Saturday	
		Time	People	Time	People	Time	People	Time	People	Time	People	Time	People	Time	People
Out of bed															
First contact with other person															
Start work/school/ Volunteer/ family care															
Dinner															
To bed															
Rate MOOD each day from -5 to +5 - 5 = very depressed +5 = very elated															

FRANK E. (2007) INTERPERSONAL AND SOCIAL RHYTHM THERAPY: A MEANS OF IMPROVING DEPRESSION AND PREVENTING RELAPSE IN BIPOLAR DISORDER. J CLIN PSYCHOL 63:463-473. REPRINTED WITH PERMISSION.

HOW TO ACE A MOOD CHART THE ellen forney WAY!

① HAVE A SPECIAL JOURNAL FOR CHARTING—

NICE & ORGANIZED → MOOD CHARTS 2018

—OR START YOUR CHART ON THE LAST PAGE OF YOUR REGULAR JOURNAL, & WORK BACKWARDS.

KEEPS LOTS OF TRACKING INFO IN ONE PLACE →

② FIGURE OUT WHAT YOU WANT TO TRACK & HOW MANY COLUMNS YOU'LL NEED.

date
meds
sleep
meals
mood
notes

THESE MAY CHANGE WITH DIFFERENT CIRCUMSTANCES.

? period? alcohol? migraines?

I LIKE HAVING A GRAB BAG "NOTES" COLUMN FOR WHO-KNOWS-WHAT, E.G. IF A RED FLAGPOLE COMES UP.

③ MAKE THE COLUMNS A GOOD WIDTH FOR WHAT YOU'LL FILL IN.

I LIKE ROOM FOR A SHORT DESCRIPTION FOR "MOOD."

Date	Meds	Hrs Sleep	Slept all night?	Reg. meals	mood	notes
11/15	200 mg Lam 2 x day	7ish	up at 3, ½ hr	✓	low in the morning but fine by noon	
11/16	"	7	✓	late breakfast	"	took day off! ☺

④ DECIDE WHEN YOU'RE GOING TO DO YOUR CHART EVERY DAY.

MORNINGS FEEL RIGHT TO ME, PLUS I CAN RECORD MY NIGHT'S SLEEP RIGHT AWAY.

OR...

DO YOU FIND THAT CHARTS ARE SOMETHING YOU'VE BEEN TOLD TO DO, & FEEL YOU SHOULD DO, BUT DON'T? SEE IF THERE'S ANOTHER WAY YOU CAN KEEP TRACK THAT SUITS YOU BETTER.

FOR EXAMPLE, IF THE THING YOU'RE REALLY CONCERNED ABOUT IS SLEEP, YOU MIGHT KEEP AN INDEX CARD & PEN IN YOUR MEDICINE CABINET, & CHART JUST THAT ONE THING IN THE MORNING.

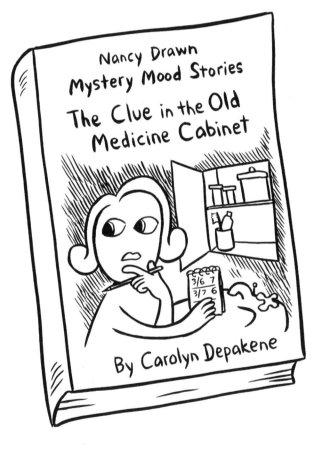

OR A VOICE MEMO ON YOUR PHONE.

OR SOMETHING.

SOME TRACKING IS BETTER THAN NO TRACKING, & MAY BE ALL YOU NEED.

CATCHING HYPOMANIA

RED FLAGS & FLAGPOLES PILED UP QUICKLY FOR ME IN SPRING, 2004. I WAS SWEPT INTO HYPOMANIA BUT MANAGED TO REEL IT IN. HERE'S A RETROSPECTIVE ANALYSIS WITH EXCERPTS FROM MY JOURNAL.

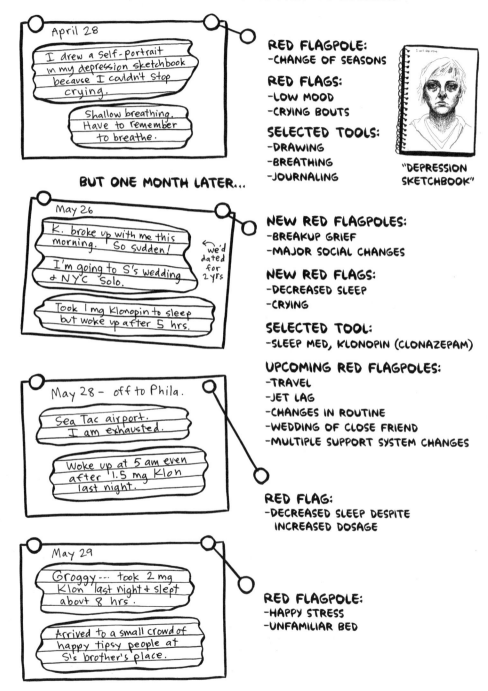

April 28

I drew a Self-portrait in my depression sketchbook because I couldn't stop crying.

Shallow breathing. Have to remember to breathe.

RED FLAGPOLE:
-CHANGE OF SEASONS

RED FLAGS:
-LOW MOOD
-CRYING BOUTS

SELECTED TOOLS:
-DRAWING
-BREATHING
-JOURNALING

"DEPRESSION SKETCHBOOK"

BUT ONE MONTH LATER...

May 26

K. broke up with me this morning. So sudden!

← we'd dated for 2 yrs

I'm going to S's wedding & NYC Solo.

Took 1 mg Klonopin to sleep but woke up after 5 hrs.

NEW RED FLAGPOLES:
-BREAKUP GRIEF
-MAJOR SOCIAL CHANGES

NEW RED FLAGS:
-DECREASED SLEEP
-CRYING

SELECTED TOOL:
-SLEEP MED, KLONOPIN (CLONAZEPAM)

UPCOMING RED FLAGPOLES:
-TRAVEL
-JET LAG
-CHANGES IN ROUTINE
-WEDDING OF CLOSE FRIEND
-MULTIPLE SUPPORT SYSTEM CHANGES

May 28 - off to Phila.

Sea Tac airport. I am exhausted.

Woke up at 5 am even after 1.5 mg Klon last night.

RED FLAG:
-DECREASED SLEEP DESPITE INCREASED DOSAGE

May 29

Groggy--- took 2 mg Klon last night & slept about 8 hrs.

Arrived to a small crowd of happy tipsy people at S's brother's place.

RED FLAGPOLE:
-HAPPY STRESS
-UNFAMILIAR BED

May 31

6½ hrs sleep. Jet lag?
Appetite↓. Sleep↓.
Mood... okay?

The wedding was lovely!

I drank a lot of white wine,
got a lot of compliments on my
beaded pink silk dress, + had a
lot of stimulating conversations.

The food was good though I
didn't eat much of it.

evening--

Emotions welled up at dinner
+ I left the restaurant in
tears. Sat in S's brother's
backyard + cried a lot +
smoked cigarettes.

RED FLAGS:
- SLEEP CONTINUES DECREASING
- ELEVATED MOOD
- DECREASED APPETITE
- INCREASED:
  - ALCOHOL CONSUMPTION &
    TOLERANCE,
  - SELF-CONFIDENCE,
  - SENSITIVITY,
  - EMOTIONALITY,
  - TALKING,
  - CIGARETTE SMOKING/
    NICOTINE CONSUMPTION

SELECTED TOOL:
- TAKING TIME OUT

June 1

New York New York
big city a dreams!

Took the Chinatown bus, sat
next to a guy with a big mop of hair
+ we talked the whole time. He
gave me his phone #. Ha!

Napped. Went to a movie.
Went to N's place. Drank scotch.

I want to go do
something gay.
A lesbian bar?

My head is
buzzing
Bzzzz

RED FLAGPOLE:
- STIMULATION OF NYC

RED FLAGS:
- INCREASED ENERGY
- INCREASED SEXUAL ENERGY
- MOOD CONTINUES ELEVATING
- SPENDING MONEY MORE EASILY
- LOOSER PERSONAL BOUNDARIES

June 3   Restless.

Found this show in Time Out +
called the Chinatown bus guy. Too
expensive for him so I decided to
treat. After the show we went to
a sake bar + walked around until
4 in the morning talking talking talking
+ smoking cigarettes, then slept in my
hotel room in our clothes (oh well).
Coffee in the morning + said good bye.
The show was great.

ADRTVV060204E

DARYL ROTH THEATRE
20 UNION SQUARE EAST, NYC

DE LA GUARDA R

PM WED

TIMEOT
$45.00
TCMSTR TM

GENADM

DARYL ROTH THEATRE
20 UNION SQUARE EAST, NYC

DE LA GUARDA R
8:00 PM WED
JUN 2, 2004

TANYS2659 0602 X23S

GENERAL ADMISSION

FORNEY, ELLEN G.

ADRTVV060204E

TIMEOT
$45.00
TCMSTR TM

GENADM

A   27

DE LA GUARDA

CALL TELECHARGE.COM 212-947-8844

102,   45. service
45. 5.50

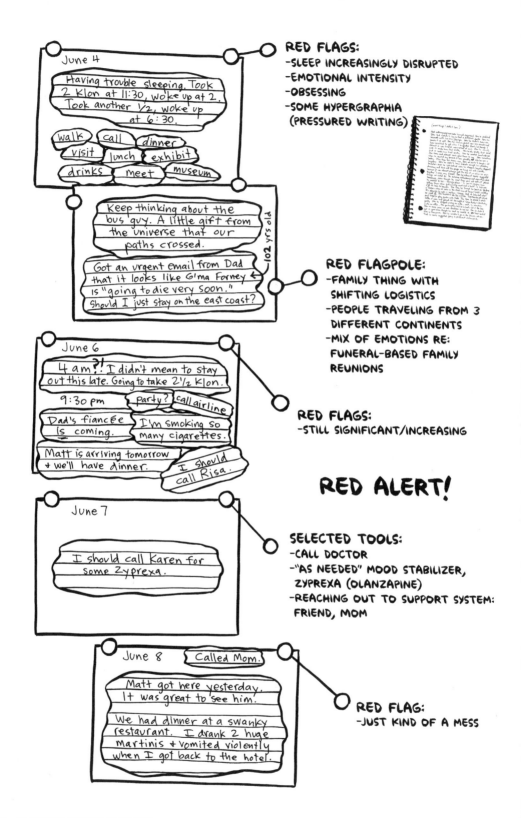

RED FLAGS:
- SLEEP INCREASINGLY DISRUPTED
- EMOTIONAL INTENSITY
- OBSESSING
- SOME HYPERGRAPHIA (PRESSURED WRITING)

June 4

Having trouble sleeping. Took 2 Klon at 11:30, woke up at 2. Took another 1/2, woke up at 6:30.

walk · call · dinner · visit · lunch · exhibit · drinks · meet · museum

Keep thinking about the bus guy. A little gift from the universe that our paths crossed.

102 yrs old

Got an urgent email from Dad that it looks like G'ma Forney is "going to die very soon." Should I just stay on the east coast?

RED FLAGPOLE:
- FAMILY THING WITH SHIFTING LOGISTICS
- PEOPLE TRAVELING FROM 3 DIFFERENT CONTINENTS
- MIX OF EMOTIONS RE: FUNERAL-BASED FAMILY REUNIONS

June 6

4 am?! I didn't mean to stay out this late. Going to take 2 1/2 Klon.

9:30 pm · party? · call airline

Dad's fiancée is coming. · I'm smoking so many cigarettes.

Matt is arriving tomorrow + we'll have dinner. · I should call Risa.

RED FLAGS:
- STILL SIGNIFICANT/INCREASING

RED ALERT!

June 7

I should call Karen for some Zyprexa.

SELECTED TOOLS:
- CALL DOCTOR
- "AS NEEDED" MOOD STABILIZER, ZYPREXA (OLANZAPINE)
- REACHING OUT TO SUPPORT SYSTEM: FRIEND, MOM

June 8 · Called Mom.

Matt got here yesterday, It was great to see him.

We had dinner at a swanky restaurant. I drank 2 huge martinis + vomited violently when I got back to the hotel.

RED FLAG:
- JUST KIND OF A MESS

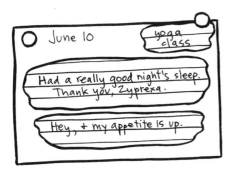

June 9

G'ma Forney died at 9:15 this morning. The funeral is on Friday.

Risa is going to pick me up at the airport when I get home.

RED FLAGPOLE STATUS:
-TRAVEL LOGISTICS MORE CLEAR
-NEARING RETURN TO ROUTINE
-SOCIAL CHANGES STILL AN ISSUE

RED FLAG STATUS:
-SLEEP INCREASING
-APPETITE INCREASING
-ENERGY SETTLING

SELECTED TOOLS:
-HELP FROM SUPPORT SYSTEM
-YOGA

June 10   yoga class

Had a really good night's sleep. Thank you, Zyprexa.

Hey, + my appetite is up.

**YEP!
STILL GOTTA
KEEP WATCH!**

June 11

We were last in line at the funeral procession + got lost. Finally found our way + said goodbye to g'ma as they were closing the tomb.

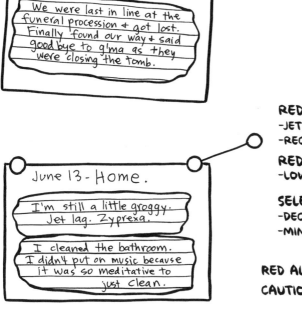

RED FLAGPOLES:
-JET LAG
-RECENT HYPOMANIA

RED FLAG:
-LOW ENERGY

SELECTED TOOLS:
-DECREASED STIMULATION
-MINDFULNESS

RED ALERT: CANCELLED.

CAUTION ADVISORY REMAINS!

June 13 - Home.

I'm still a little groggy. Jet lag. Zyprexa.

I cleaned the bathroom. I didn't put on music because it was so meditative to just clean.

IF YOUR RED FLAGS GET INTO THE REALM OF
SUICIDAL THOUGHTS,
YOU ARE NOT ALONE.

"LIVE THROUGH THIS" IS A POWERFUL ONLINE PORTRAIT SERIES OF SUICIDE ATTEMPT SURVIVORS & THEIR STORIES.

BY CREATING THAT PORTRAIT SERIES,

I learned that I'm **not alone.**

It's what I set out to show other people, & it taught me the same thing.

It might seem like you will never get to the other side, like the pain will never be bearable, but you will get to the other side.

Step by step.

Breath by breath.

*

I thought I was a burden to everyone who loves me.

The reality was that everyone cared — I just couldn't see it.

DESE'RAE L. STAGE
PHOTOGRAPHER, WRITER, SUICIDE ATTEMPT SURVIVOR, LIVING WITH BIPOLAR

LIVE THROUGH THIS

97 STRONG & MORE IN PROGRESS.
LIVETHROUGHTHIS.ORG

KEVIN HINES
SUICIDE ATTEMPT SURVIVOR, MENTAL HEALTH ADVOCATE, LIVING WITH BIPOLAR

"THE GUY WHO JUMPED OFF THE GOLDEN GATE BRIDGE & SURVIVED TO TELL HIS STORY" = A SHORT VERSION OF HIS STORY ON YOUTUBE

If you're suffering mentally, don't wait like I did, sitting in denial for so long. Because recovery happens.

*EXCERPTS FROM "23 MESSAGES FOR ANYONE CONSIDERING SUICIDE, FROM PEOPLE WHO HAVE BEEN THERE" THEMIGHTY.COM, 1-20-2016

"SUICIDAL IDEATION" MAY MEAN ANYTHING FROM OCCASIONAL THOUGHTS, TO PLANNING OR ACTING IN A SUICIDAL CRISIS.

SOME THINGS YOU CAN DO

• DISTRESS TOLERANCE SKILLS

DIALECTICAL BEHAVIOR THERAPY SPECIFICALLY ADDRESSES SELF-HARM & SUICIDAL THOUGHTS, & HOW TO MANAGE THEM IN BOTH THE SHORT & LONG TERM. SOME OF THE SKILLS ARE IN CHAPTER 3 (E.G. MINDFULNESS, BREATHING, MUSIC) & THERE ARE MANY, MANY MORE. LOOK INTO DBT &/OR SEARCH "DISTRESS TOLERANCE SKILLS."

YOU DON'T NEED TO WAIT FOR A CRISIS --

REACH OUT.

CALL THE
• NATIONAL SUICIDE PREVENTION LIFELINE
(EVEN JUST FOR NON-CRISIS SUPPORT!)

(800) 273-8255
Nat'l Suicide Prevention Helpline

1   2 ABC   3 DEF

FOR OTHER HOTLINES - LGBTQ, HEARING IMPAIRED, TEEN - SEE RESOURCES AT THE END OF THIS BOOK

• CALL OR CONNECT WITH SOMEONE IN YOUR SUPPORT SYSTEM

• ASK A FRIEND OR FAMILY MEMBER TO STAY WITH YOU FOR A WHILE

• TALK WITH YOUR DOCTOR ABOUT YOUR MEDS & IF THEY NEED TO BE ADJUSTED OR CHANGED

IF YOU'RE IN CRISIS,
• GET YOURSELF SAFE.

GO (OR IDEALLY, ASK SOMEONE TO TAKE YOU) TO THE ER

CALL 9-1-1 & SAY IT'S A MENTAL HEALTH EMERGENCY

STABILIZE WITH A VOLUNTARY STAY ON AN INPATIENT PSYCH UNIT

ALLISON, A VOLUNTEER WITH NAMI SEATTLE, TALKED WITH ME ABOUT HER VOLUNTARY STAY ON AN INPATIENT PSYCHIATRIC UNIT.

ONE WEEK BEFORE CHRISTMAS, 2015. ALLISON WASN'T EATING OR SLEEPING. SHE THOUGHT SHE WAS A PREGNANT ANGEL.

I am in an alternate universe of kundalini rising

--- I am a gift

HOUSESITTING

THEN IT ALL TOOK A DARK SPIN. HER ALTERNATE UNIVERSE STARTED TO FEEL LIKE "THE TRUMAN SHOW."*

I can't slow down

Something is really wrong

SHE CALLED HER MOTHER, AUNTS, & THERAPIST, & THEY TOOK HER TO THE ER.

SOON... SHE WAS ADMITTED TO THE TWO EAST INPATIENT UNIT AT SWEDISH HOSPITAL.

BEING DETAINED & CONSTANTLY UNDER SURVEILLANCE WAS JARRING. LOTS OF THINGS WERE UNHELPFUL...

CLINICAL COLDNESS OF THE STAFF

Shaky hands? Delusions? No? Great – I'll check in tomorrow.

Wait— ch!

NO PHYSICAL EXERCISE

What happened? What do I do now?

BUT MOSTLY, FEELING POWERLESS & UNINFORMED

& LOTS OF THINGS WERE HELPFUL.

SLEEPING   EATING   DRINKING WATER

TIME

CAMARADERIE WITH OTHER PATIENTS

feels

Are you cold? I'm cold.

wanna borrow my hoodie?

lasting friendship

FEELING STRIPPED OF PRETENSE

UNSELFCONSCIOUSLY → BEDRAGGLED

STABILIZING

AFTER SIX DAYS, SHE DECIDED SHE WAS READY TO LEAVE. HER BROTHERS CAME TO PICK HER UP.

You'll be leaving against medical advice. We strongly recommend that you stay.

I know. What do I need to sign?

YEARS LATER, SHE DOESN'T REGRET LEAVING. BUT SHE DOESN'T REGRET HER STAY, EITHER.

I'm still here.

...& A NAMI SPEAKER!

*THE MOVIE, I.E. FEELING PARANOID & DISORIENTED

SUBSTANCES
...A LOADED ISSUE

WE HAVE A SITUATION. AT LEAST HALF OF PEOPLE WITH MOOD DISORDERS PARTAKE - MOSTLY ALCOHOL OR POT. IT'S A PROBLEM FOR SOME PEOPLE MORE THAN OTHERS, BUT IT'S A RISK FOR ALL OF US.*

"RISK" MEANING POTENTIALLY COMPROMISING:

☆ YOUR PHYSICAL HEALTH,

☆ THE EFFECTIVENESS OF YOUR THERAPY & MEDS,

☆ YOUR ABILITY TO TELL THE DIFFERENCE BETWEEN YOUR SYMPTOMS & THE EFFECTS OF SUBSTANCES,

☆ YOUR ABILITY TO HANDLE DIFFICULT EMOTIONS (I.E., CONSCIOUSLY OR SUBCONSCIOUSLY AVOIDING THEM), OR

☆ ADDICTION.

IF YOU'RE **SOBER** BY PREFERENCE, CHOICE, OR NECESSITY, YOU'RE ON THE MOST RELIABLE PATH FOR KEEPING YOUR MIND & BODY HEALTHY & STABLE. THIS IS ESPECIALLY THE PATH FOR PEOPLE WITH PARTICULARLY FINE-TUNED OR FRAGILE BRAINS OR ADDICTIVE TENDENCIES.

*PLEASE NOTE THAT I'M NOT INCLUDING MEDICAL CANNABIS SPECIFICALLY, THOUGH THERE'S OVERLAP IN SOME ISSUES, ESPECIALLY IF YOU'RE "PRESCRIBING" FOR YOURSELF.

HOWEVER, FOR THOSE WHO ACKNOWLEDGE THE RISKS & DO PARTAKE, THERE'S A CONTINUUM FROM

MAYBE OKAY TO **PROBABLY A PROBLEM** TO **DEFINITELY A PROBLEM**

So how do you know if it's a problem?

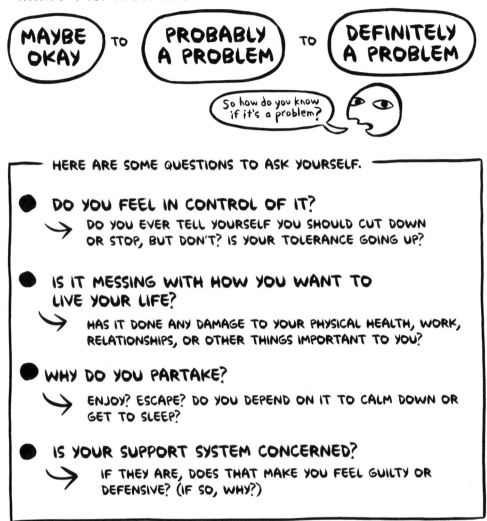

HERE ARE SOME QUESTIONS TO ASK YOURSELF.

● **DO YOU FEEL IN CONTROL OF IT?**
  → DO YOU EVER TELL YOURSELF YOU SHOULD CUT DOWN OR STOP, BUT DON'T? IS YOUR TOLERANCE GOING UP?

● **IS IT MESSING WITH HOW YOU WANT TO LIVE YOUR LIFE?**
  → HAS IT DONE ANY DAMAGE TO YOUR PHYSICAL HEALTH, WORK, RELATIONSHIPS, OR OTHER THINGS IMPORTANT TO YOU?

● **WHY DO YOU PARTAKE?**
  → ENJOY? ESCAPE? DO YOU DEPEND ON IT TO CALM DOWN OR GET TO SLEEP?

● **IS YOUR SUPPORT SYSTEM CONCERNED?**
  → IF THEY ARE, DOES THAT MAKE YOU FEEL GUILTY OR DEFENSIVE? (IF SO, WHY?)

IF YOU'RE CERTAIN IT'S JUST SOMETHING ENJOYABLE, RELATIVELY INFREQUENT, AND NOT GETTING YOU OR YOUR LIFE EFFED UP – & YOU'RE SURE YOU'RE BEING HONEST WITH YOURSELF – IT

→ **MAY BE OKAY.** ←

IT'S STILL A RISK, THOUGH. STAY AWARE, & DO GIVE IT A REST WHEN YOUR MOODS ARE PROBLEMATIC OR WHEN YOU NOTICE ANY RED FLAGS OR FLAGPOLES.

IF IT'S MESSING WITH YOUR LIFE A BIT, BUT YOU HAVEN'T STOPPED FOR SOME REASON, IT'S

→ | PROBABLY A PROBLEM. | ←

MAKE SURE YOU CAN GET SOBER OR REIN IT IN. IF YOU'RE NOT READY OR DON'T WANT TO STOP, MAYBE YOU NEED TO DETOX A BIT, PARTAKE LESS, OR START TAKING STEPS TOWARD GIVING IT UP COMPLETELY. THINGS TO DO, FOR ANY OF THOSE OPTIONS:

PAY ATTENTION AND KEEP TRACK.

- FIGURE OUT HOW OFTEN & HOW MUCH YOU'RE PARTAKING. WRITE IT DOWN (& OF COURSE THERE ARE APPS FOR THIS!).

- KNOW WHICH SITUATIONS TEND TOWARD YOUR PARTAKING IMPULSIVELY OR TOO MUCH (LIKE SOCIALIZING WITH CERTAIN FRIENDS, HANGING OUT ALONE AT HOME, ETC.).

MAKE A PLAN THAT IS REALISTIC AND CONSISTENT WITH YOUR VALUES.

- GIVE YOURSELF SOME YOU-SPECIFIC GOALS & LIMITS – AMOUNT, FREQUENCY, & CONTEXT.

REDUCE YOUR AMOUNT.

- WHATEVER HELPS YOU STICK TO YOUR GOALS, DO THAT. SOLID SELF-CONGRATS, TAKING NOTE OF HEALTH BENEFITS, &/OR CHECK-INS WITH YOUR DOCTOR OR SOMEONE IN YOUR SUPPORT SYSTEM.

- HAVE STRATEGIES TO DEAL WITH THE SITUATIONS THAT HAVE BEEN TROUBLE. MAYBE YOU CAN AVOID THEM, OR PLAN TO LEAVE EARLY, OR HAVE A LINE THAT YOU CAN REPEAT.

- IF IT'S A SOCIAL ISSUE, LET YOUR FRIENDS KNOW AHEAD OF TIME THAT YOU HAVE CERTAIN LIMITS. MAYBE THEY CAN HELP REMIND YOU, OR THEY CAN AT LEAST NOT OFFER YOU WHAT YOU'RE LIMITING.

IF YOU'VE TRIED TO BRING IT INTO YOUR CONTROL & IT HASN'T WORKED, IT'S

→ DEFINITELY A PROBLEM. ←

MAYBE YOU'VE BEEN AVOIDING SOME ISSUE & WOULD BE BETTER SERVED BY DEALING WITH IT SOME OTHER WAY, OR MAYBE AT THIS POINT YOU'D BE RISKING WITHDRAWALS TO GO OFF ON YOUR OWN.

TAKING CHARGE OF THE SITUATION BASICALLY MEANS REACHING OUT FOR HELP.

HERE ARE SOME OPTIONS:

- TALK TO YOUR DOCTOR, IF YOU HAVEN'T ALREADY – YOUR FAMILY DOCTOR OR YOUR THERAPIST. SEE IF YOU CAN FIND AN ADDICTION SPECIALIST, ESPECIALLY AN ADDICTION PSYCHIATRIST.

- REACH OUT TO YOUR SUPPORT SYSTEM FOR HELP FIGURING OUT WHAT TO DO, GETTING THAT PROCESS STARTED, & SUPPORTING YOU THROUGH IT.

- CHECK OUT INFORMATION, TREATMENT OPTIONS, & LINKS TO RESOURCES ON THE NAMI OR AMERICAN SOCIETY OF ADDICTION MEDICINE WEBSITES.

- IF YOU'RE REALLY FEELING OUT OF CONTROL, "TREATMENT OPTIONS" MAY MEAN GETTING TO THE E.R., OR CHECKING IN TO REHAB.

THE PSYCHIATRISTS I CONFERRED WITH ABOUT SUBSTANCES WERE ADAMANT THAT WE NEED TO BE OPEN WITH OUR DOCTORS ABOUT ANY SUBSTANCES WE USE, THAT THEY CAN'T HELP A PATIENT IF THEY DON'T KNOW WHAT THEY'RE UP TO. FAIR ENOUGH.

BUT REALLY. IF WE'RE EXPENDING ALL THAT TIME, ENERGY, & MONEY TO GET HELP & GUIDANCE, IT DOESN'T SERVE US WELL TO NOT BE OPEN.

IF WE CAN'T TRUST OUR DOCTORS, OR IF THEY'RE MORE CONSERVATIVE THAN WE CLICK WITH- MORE "ALL-OR-NOTHING"- THEY MAY BE TOO CONSERVATIVE IN OTHER WAYS, TOO.

WE NEED TO BE

SELF-AWARE, REALISTIC, & EFFECTIVE.

IF SUBSTANCES ARE AN ISSUE, THAT NEEDS TO BE IN THE SCOPE OF OUR TREATMENT, JUST AS OUR MOOD DISORDERS ARE.

SOME THINGS TO REMEMBER ABOUT MANIA

ESPECIALLY IF YOU FEEL LIKE YOU MISS IT, OR NEED IT.

MANIA HAS UNDENIABLY
APPEALING ASPECTS.
POWERFUL. NO QUESTION.

BUT THOSE SAME ASPECTS HAVE FLIP
SIDES THAT SUCK EVEN AT THE TIME,
& CAN BE DEVASTATING LATER.

NOT SLEEPING	MORE TIME TO LIVE LIVE LIVE!	BODY IS DEPLETED & EXHAUSTED
NOT EATING	FEELING SVELTE!	
OVERFLOWING ENERGY	CHARISMA! INTENSITY! SELF-CONFIDENCE!	EXPLOSIVE, PUSHING AWAY YOUR PEOPLE
SPENDING MONEY EASILY	MONEY IS NO OBJECT! GREAT STUFF EVERYWHERE!	BIG DEBT, BAD CREDIT, QUESTIONABLE VALUE OF "GREAT STUFF"
BIG PLANS	BRILLIANCE! VAST POSSIBILITIES!	BURNED BRIDGES, FALLOUT FROM IMPULSIVE MAJOR DECISIONS
REALLY SEX-DRIVEN	HOT!	OBSESSIVE, INSATIABLE, RISKY

FEELS LIKE IT WILL LAST
FOREVER!

NOPE. IS ACTUALLY,
INEVITABLY, FOLLOWED BY
DEPRESSION

IT'S EASY TO ROMANTICIZE MANIA WHEN YOU HAVEN'T
EXPERIENCED IT FOR A WHILE. IT'S PRACTICALLY IMPOSSIBLE TO
REMEMBER HOW HARD THE FALL IS AFTERWARDS, OR HOW
CRUSHING THE DEPRESSION IS AFTER THAT (& DEPRESSION
USUALLY STICKS AROUND MUCH LONGER THAN MANIA).

TALK WITH YOUR FRIENDS. REREAD YOUR JOURNAL.
YOU HAVE PERSPECTIVE WHEN YOU'RE STABLE.
TAKE ADVANTAGE OF THAT!

THE BIG THING TO REMEMBER
ABOUT
DEPRESSION:

I HAD A THREAD OF LOGIC THAT
ALLOWED ME TO HOLD ON TO SOME HOPE.

HANG IN THERE.

MERIT BADGES
FOR THE
DANGER ZONE

PREDICTED

RECOGNIZED

PREVENTED

CAUGHT

KNOW
YOUR RED
FLAGPOLES

KNOW YOUR
RED FLAGS

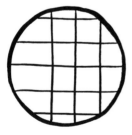

MOOD CHART

AWARENESS +
CONTROL OF
SUBSTANCE ISSUES

RESPECT
YOURSELF NO
MATTER WHAT

CHAPTER 7
YOU HAVE COMPANY

☆ YOU ARE NOT ALONE, & YOU ARE NOT ALONE IN FEELING ALONE. ☆

THE COLD, HARD STATISTICS ARE CLEAR: BIPOLAR DISORDER IS PRETTY COMMON, DEPRESSION IS **REALLY** COMMON, & MENTAL ILLNESS OVERALL IS **TOTALLY** COMMON.

☆ ABOUT 3% OF THE POPULATION HAS BIPOLAR DISORDER,

☆ ABOUT 10% HAS SOME SORT OF MOOD DISORDER, &

☆ ABOUT 18% HAS SOME SORT OF MENTAL ILLNESS.

Well then, why do I _feel_ so alone?

WELL, STATISTICS ARE ONLY SO HELPFUL.

THE BEST WAY TO REALLY FEEL THAT YOU'RE NOT ALONE IS TO FIND LIKE-MINDED PEOPLE OR THEIR STORIES.

NATIONAL INSTITUTE OF MENTAL HEALTH, 2015.

IT'S NOT ACTUALLY THAT HARD TO

⭐ FIND LIKE-MINDED PEOPLE'S STORIES & WORDS.

● READ

MEMOIRS

MARBLES
MANIA, DEPRESSION, MICHELANGELO, & ME
ELLEN FORNEY

WILLIAM STYRON
DARKNESS VISIBLE

CARRIE FISHER
Shockaholic

AN UNQUIET MIND
KAY REDFIELD JAMISON

esperanza
cope with anxiety & depression

bp MAGAZINE
Routine Matters
LOVE OR MANIA?
Symptoms As Strengths
SHELBY TWETEN

COURAGE TO CHANGE
HOWIE MANDEL

MANY MORE MEMOIRS IN THE HALL OF FAME, IN A FEW PAGES!

MAGAZINES

● LISTEN

MUSIC

"I've got bipolar disorder my shit's not in order"

MARY LAMBERT "SECRETS"

"Listed as manic depressive with extreme paranoia Hey dog, I got something for ya"

DMX "FUCKIN' WIT' D"

"I went tumbling down tryna reach your high"

HALSEY "DEVIL IN ME"

"Baby I've been low but never this low"

BRUCE SPRINGSTEEN, "THIS DEPRESSION"

PODCASTS

THE MENTAL ILLNESS Happy Hour

THE HILARIOUS WORLD OF DEPRESSION

RADIOLAB
8-23-15 "LITHIUM"

FRESH AIR
10-24-16 INTERVIEW WITH COMIC CHRIS GETHARD

JUST A SAMPLING OF...

THINGS TO WATCH & PERUSE

Lady Dynamite	WISHFUL DRINKING	RIDE THE TIGER
MARIA BAMFORD'S NETFLIX SHOW	CARRIE FISHER'S ONE-WOMAN SHOW	STREAMING PBS DOCUMENTARY

DOCUMENTARIES

MIND | GAME THE UNQUIET JOURNEY OF CHAMIQUE HOLDSCLAW	Stephen Fry: THE SECRET LIFE OF THE MANIC DEPRESSIVE	BEYOND SILENCE
PROFILES FORMER WNBA STAR WITH BIPOLAR	EMMY-WINNER; INTERVIEWS WITH CELEBS WITH BIPOLAR	3 PROFILES; EXECUTIVE PRODUCER DEMI LOVATO

WEBSITES

nami NATIONAL ALLIANCE ON MENTAL ILLNESS	DBSA DEPRESSION & BIPOLAR SUPPORT ALLIANCE	bring change to mind
INFO INCLUDES VIDEO INTERVIEWS WITH PEOPLE OF COLOR: NAMI.ORG	INFO INCLUDES "LIFE UNLIMITED" PERSONAL STORIES: DBSALLIANCE.ORG	LOTS OF INFO & PERSONAL STORIES: BRINGCHANGE2MIND.ORG

WEBSITES & MESSAGE BOARDS

The MIGHTY	Psych Central*	Crazy Boards*
ARTICLES & PERSONAL STORIES: THEMIGHTY.COM	POPULAR MESSAGE BOARD: PSYCHCENTRAL.COM	POPULAR MESSAGE BOARD: CRAZYBOARDS.ORG

*MENTAL ADVISORY! REMEMBER, EVERYONE'S EXPERIENCE IS DIFFERENT, & YOU KNOW VERY LITTLE ABOUT THE PERSON POSTING.

⭐ FIND LIKE-MINDED PEOPLE, IN PERSON.

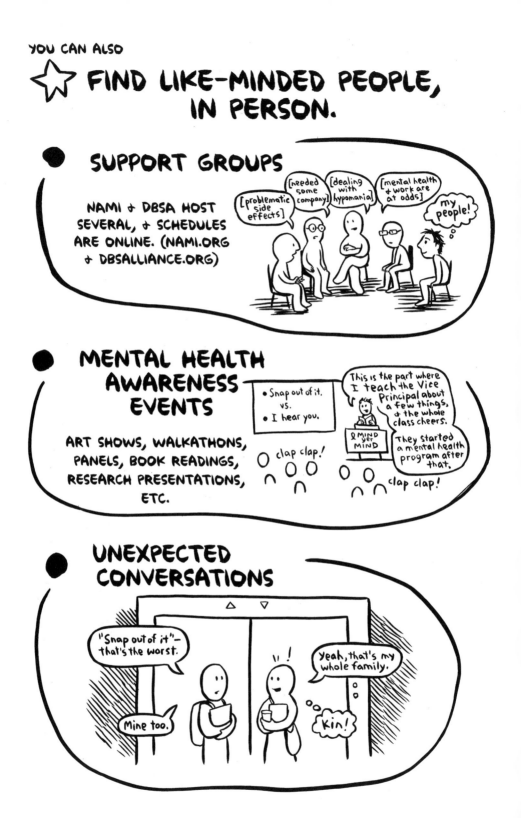

● SUPPORT GROUPS

NAMI & DBSA HOST SEVERAL, & SCHEDULES ARE ONLINE. (NAMI.ORG & DBSALLIANCE.ORG)

[problematic side effects]

[needed some company]

[dealing with hypomania]

[mental health & work are at odds]

my people!

● MENTAL HEALTH AWARENESS EVENTS

ART SHOWS, WALKATHONS, PANELS, BOOK READINGS, RESEARCH PRESENTATIONS, ETC.

• Snap out of it.
vs.
• I hear you.

clap clap!

This is the part where I teach the Vice Principal about a few things, & the whole class cheers.

MIND yer MIND

They started a mental health program after that.

clap clap!

● UNEXPECTED CONVERSATIONS

"Snap out of it"— that's the worst.

Mine too.

!

Yeah, that's my whole family.

Kin!

⭐ COMING OUT, PRIVATELY OR PUBLICLY, SOFTLY OR WITH A MEGAPHONE, IS UP TO YOU.

YOU DON'T HAVE TO...

...BUT THERE ARE PLENTY OF REASONS TO COME OUT. LIKE, YOU CAN--

● GET SUPPORT EMOTIONALLY--   ● & LOGISTICALLY

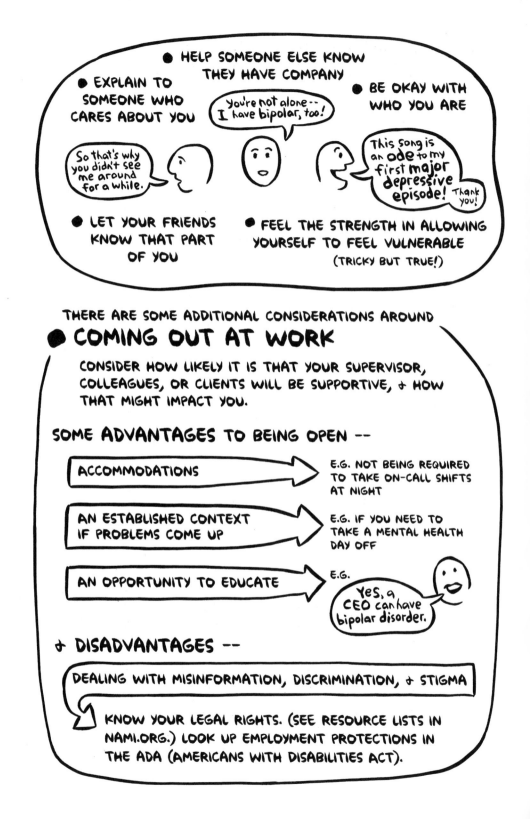

- **HELP SOMEONE ELSE KNOW THEY HAVE COMPANY**

- **EXPLAIN TO SOMEONE WHO CARES ABOUT YOU**

You're not alone -- I have bipolar, too!

- **BE OKAY WITH WHO YOU ARE**

So that's why you didn't see me around for a while.

This song is an ode to my first major depressive episode! Thank you!

- **LET YOUR FRIENDS KNOW THAT PART OF YOU**

- **FEEL THE STRENGTH IN ALLOWING YOURSELF TO FEEL VULNERABLE** (TRICKY BUT TRUE!)

THERE ARE SOME ADDITIONAL CONSIDERATIONS AROUND

● COMING OUT AT WORK

CONSIDER HOW LIKELY IT IS THAT YOUR SUPERVISOR, COLLEAGUES, OR CLIENTS WILL BE SUPPORTIVE, & HOW THAT MIGHT IMPACT YOU.

SOME ADVANTAGES TO BEING OPEN --

ACCOMMODATIONS → E.G. NOT BEING REQUIRED TO TAKE ON-CALL SHIFTS AT NIGHT

AN ESTABLISHED CONTEXT IF PROBLEMS COME UP → E.G. IF YOU NEED TO TAKE A MENTAL HEALTH DAY OFF

AN OPPORTUNITY TO EDUCATE → E.G. *Yes, a CEO can have bipolar disorder.*

& DISADVANTAGES --

DEALING WITH MISINFORMATION, DISCRIMINATION, & STIGMA

KNOW YOUR LEGAL RIGHTS. (SEE RESOURCE LISTS IN NAMI.ORG.) LOOK UP EMPLOYMENT PROTECTIONS IN THE ADA (AMERICANS WITH DISABILITIES ACT).

IF IT FEELS OVERWHELMING, HERE ARE A FEW

COMING-OUT SUGGESTIONS:

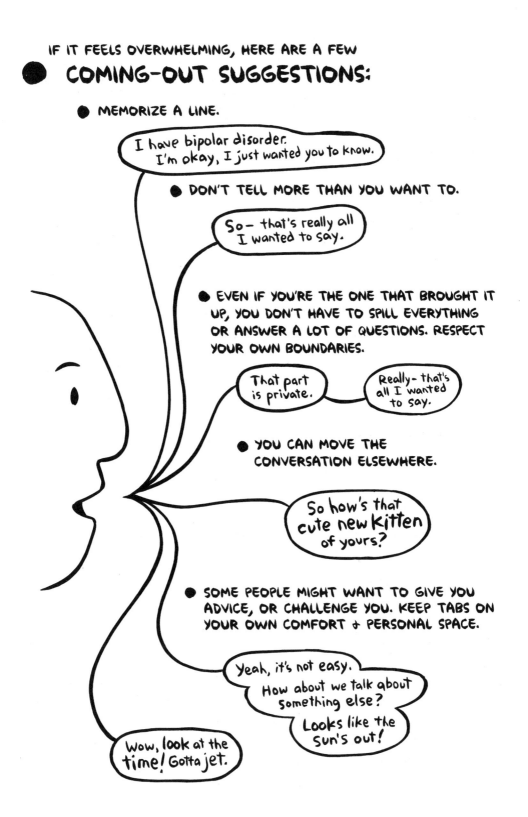

- MEMORIZE A LINE.

I have bipolar disorder. I'm okay, I just wanted you to know.

- DON'T TELL MORE THAN YOU WANT TO.

So— that's really all I wanted to say.

- EVEN IF YOU'RE THE ONE THAT BROUGHT IT UP, YOU DON'T HAVE TO SPILL EVERYTHING OR ANSWER A LOT OF QUESTIONS. RESPECT YOUR OWN BOUNDARIES.

That part is private.

Really— that's all I wanted to say.

- YOU CAN MOVE THE CONVERSATION ELSEWHERE.

So how's that cute new kitten of yours?

- SOME PEOPLE MIGHT WANT TO GIVE YOU ADVICE, OR CHALLENGE YOU. KEEP TABS ON YOUR OWN COMFORT & PERSONAL SPACE.

Yeah, it's not easy. How about we talk about something else? Looks like the sun's out!

Wow, look at the time! Gotta jet.

Mind Your Manners Because Your Mind Matters!

ASK...

THE BIPOLAR MZ. MANNERS

DEAR BIPOLAR MZ. MANNERS:

WHAT IS THE ETIQUETTE FOR TELLING SOMEONE YOU'RE DATING THAT YOU HAVE A MOOD DISORDER?

— TOTALLY LOVE CRAZY

DEAR TLC,

I DISCUSSED THIS VERY QUESTION WITH SEX ADVICE EXPERT DAN SAVAGE ON HIS SAVAGE LOVECAST. THERE ARE STRIKING SIMILARITIES WITH TELLING A NEW LOVE INTEREST ABOUT YOUR KINKS! THE FOLLOWING IS MY BIPOLAR MZ. MANNERS VERSION OF HIS ADVICE.

♡ BE CALM & SOBER, & IDEALLY, STABLE.

♡ GIVE YOUR DISCLOSURE THE TIME, SPACE, & CARE IT DESERVES.

♡ IT'S FINE TO WAIT & GET TO KNOW EACH OTHER FIRST. IF YOU DON'T CLICK, IT'S A MOOT POINT!

♡ IT'S ALSO OKAY TO DISCLOSE RIGHT AWAY IF YOU WANT TO VET THEM, BUT ONLY IF YOU'RE CONFIDENT YOU'D BE OKAY WITH A REJECTION.

♡ OH, LET'S SAY, 2-5 DATES.

♡ DO DISCLOSE BEFORE MAKING ANY MAJOR COMMITMENTS.

♡ A CAUTION IF YOU'RE FEELING SUPER-HIGH-ENERGY SEXUAL: ENTANGLING WHILE MANIC CAN MAKE FOR FRAYED KNOTS!

BEST WISHES FOR GETTING THE LOVE YOU DESERVE!

IN SOLIDARITY,

the Bipolar Mz. Manners ♡

I ADMIT, I WASN'T SO CAUTIOUS ABOUT TELLING THIS GUY...

I MET JAKE WHILE I WAS VISITING PORTLAND IN 2009. I PURSUED HIM TIRELESSLY FOR THREE DAYS.

teaching a workshop
PNCA
yur's
beerz
Doug Fir
c'mere!
I think you're great!
eek!
actually bicycles

HE FINALLY GAVE IN, & I TOTALLY FELL FOR HIM.

smak!
yay!
I said this for real.

LATER, IN MY HOTEL ROOM...

Should I take my meds fast, so he doesn't see?
Or wait until he comes out, & act like it's no big deal?

shk~ sshkreek!
his shower is over

I COULD NOT DECIDE QUICKLY ENOUGH. THUS, I SUCCEEDED AT NEITHER.

These are just...
I'm bipolar.

I SUPPOSE PART OF ME JUST WANTED TO GET IT OVER WITH.

If he's gonna bolt, best that he do it now!

ding dong

No big deal.
Remember, I went to art school.

AS VIEWED IN OH-MY-GOD STRESS-O-VISION

WE SURVIVED THAT AND BECAME PARTNERS. NINE YEARS LATER, IT'S A STORY WE TELL.

JAKE HAS THE LAST LINE:

I admit it made me nervous.
Not the bipolar part— the blurt part!

"ONE OF THE THINGS THAT BAFFLES ME (& THERE ARE QUITE A FEW) IS HOW THERE CAN BE SO MUCH LINGERING STIGMA WITH REGARDS TO MENTAL ILLNESS, SPECIFICALLY BIPOLAR DISORDER. IN MY OPINION, LIVING WITH MANIC DEPRESSION TAKES A TREMENDOUS AMOUNT OF BALLS."

– CARRIE FISHER

"PEOPLE GET REALLY IRRITATED BY MENTAL ILLNESS."

– MARIA BAMFORD

OH, STIGMA.

SO MUCH OF OUR MENTAL HEALTH REVOLVES AROUND STIGMA – WHAT TREATMENT IS AVAILABLE, AFFORDABLE, & SUSTAINABLE... THE SUPPORT WE DO OR DON'T GET... EVEN JUST WHAT IT MEANS TO BE WHO WE ARE & GO ABOUT OUR LIVES.

WHAT DOES THAT MEAN, ANYWAY —

"THE STIGMA OF
MENTAL ILLNESS" —?

THERE'S ——

PUBLIC STIGMA

— THE NEGATIVE STEREOTYPES THAT MAKE SOME
PEOPLE AVOID OR FEAR US (WHICH CAN EVEN
INCLUDE OUR OWN COMMUNITIES & FAMILY),

& THE DISCRIMINATION THAT
GOES ALONG WITH THAT (AT
WORK, SCHOOL, LEGISLATION,
ETC. BLAH BLAH BLARGH)

THE MOST COMMON MYTHS
ABOUT MENTAL ILLNESS

DEAR READER, PLEASE JAB AT THIS
DRAWING WITH YOUR FINGER & SAY
NOPE, YOU ARE WRONG.

& ## SELF-STIGMA

— THE SHAME & LOW SELF-
RESPECT THAT COMES WITH
INTERNALIZING PUBLIC STIGMA.

STIGMA CAN ALSO BE COMPOUNDED WHEN IT'S
COMBINED WITH OTHER STEREOTYPES.

MEN TEND TO FEEL PRESSURE TO NOT SEEM WEAK, &
PEOPLE IN GROUPS ALREADY CONTENDING WITH RACISM
& OTHER SETS OF RESTRICTIVE CULTURAL NORMS ARE
LESS LIKELY TO GET SUPPORT OR SEEK HELP.

IT SUUUCKS. BUT DON'T LET IT STOP YOU!

EYE ON THE PRIZE: AN END TO DISCRIMINATION IN INSTITUTIONS & THE GENERAL PUBLIC. IN THE MEANTIME, HERE ARE SOME PERSON-SIZED

STIGMA SQUASHERS

⭐ **TELL YOUR STORY.**

BEING OUT IS THE BEST WAY TO COUNTERACT BOTH PUBLIC & SELF-STIGMA. TALK, WRITE, PARTICIPATE IN AWARENESS EVENTS, EMBRACE RANDOM OPPORTUNITIES.

⭐ **CALL OUT NASTY STEREOTYPES.**

TALK OR WRITE ABOUT CRINGE-WORTHY DEPICTIONS IN MOVIES OR THE MEDIA. CHALLENGE THEM WHEN THEY POP UP.

⭐ **KNOW STUFF.**

FACTS, NEWS, LEGISLATION.

⭐ **ADVOCATE.**

CONTACT YOUR REPRESENTATIVES ABOUT LEGISLATION THAT IMPACTS MENTAL HEALTH.

⭐ **EDUCATE.**

SUGGEST OR ORGANIZE AN AWARENESS WEEK WORKSHOP, REACH OUT TO COMMUNITY LEADERS & BE AWARE OF CULTURE-SPECIFIC ISSUES. WEAR A LIME GREEN AWARENESS ACCESSORY.

⭐ **DO SOME ARTS THING.**

PUT TOGETHER AN ANTHOLOGY, CURATE AN ART SHOW, VOLUNTEER AT AN EVENT.

 SUPPORT MENTAL HEALTH ORGANIZATIONS.

VOLUNTEER, DONATE, FUNDRAISE, RECOMMEND, PROMOTE, LINK.

IMPORTANT NOTE! THESE ARE NOT SHOULDS! THEY ARE OPTIONS.

EVEN IF YOU DON'T THINK YOU KNOW ANYONE WITH A MOOD DISORDER, THERE ARE LOTS OF ACCOMPLISHED, INSPIRING, FAMOUS & REGULAR PEOPLE WITH MOOD DISORDERS WHO ARE OUT & THRIVING.

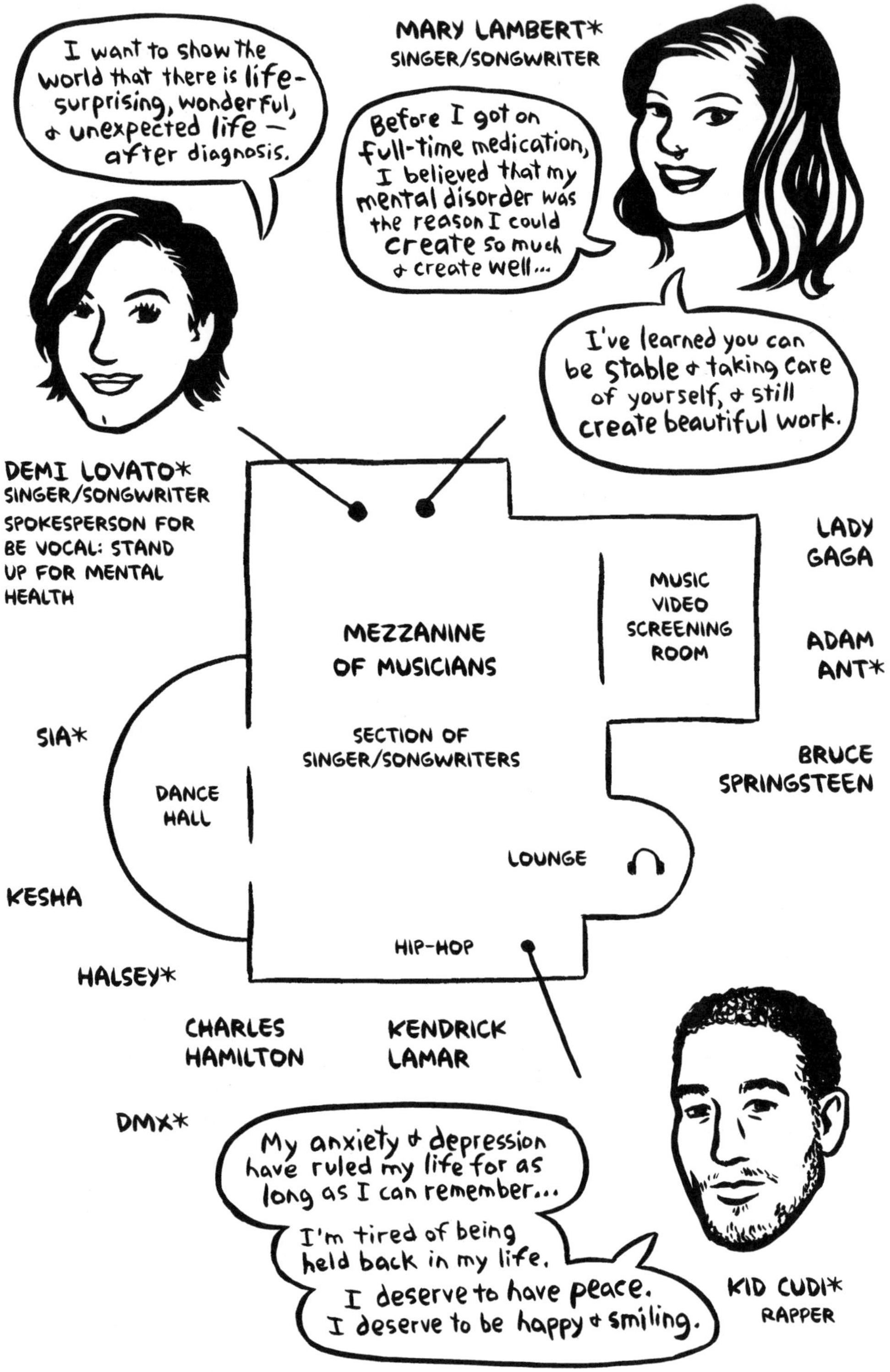
I want to show the world that there is life- surprising, wonderful, & unexpected life - after diagnosis.
DEMI LOVATO*
SINGER/SONGWRITER
SPOKESPERSON FOR BE VOCAL: STAND UP FOR MENTAL HEALTH
MARY LAMBERT*
SINGER/SONGWRITER
Before I got on full-time medication, I believed that my mental disorder was the reason I could create so much & create well...
I've learned you can be stable & taking care of yourself, & still create beautiful work.
MEZZANINE OF MUSICIANS
MUSIC VIDEO SCREENING ROOM
SECTION OF SINGER/SONGWRITERS
DANCE HALL
LOUNGE
HIP-HOP
LADY GAGA
ADAM ANT*
BRUCE SPRINGSTEEN
SIA*
KESHA
HALSEY*
CHARLES HAMILTON
KENDRICK LAMAR
DMX*
My anxiety & depression have ruled my life for as long as I can remember...
I'm tired of being held back in my life.
I deserve to have peace. I deserve to be happy & smiling.
KID CUDI*
RAPPER

*DIAGNOSED WITH BIPOLAR

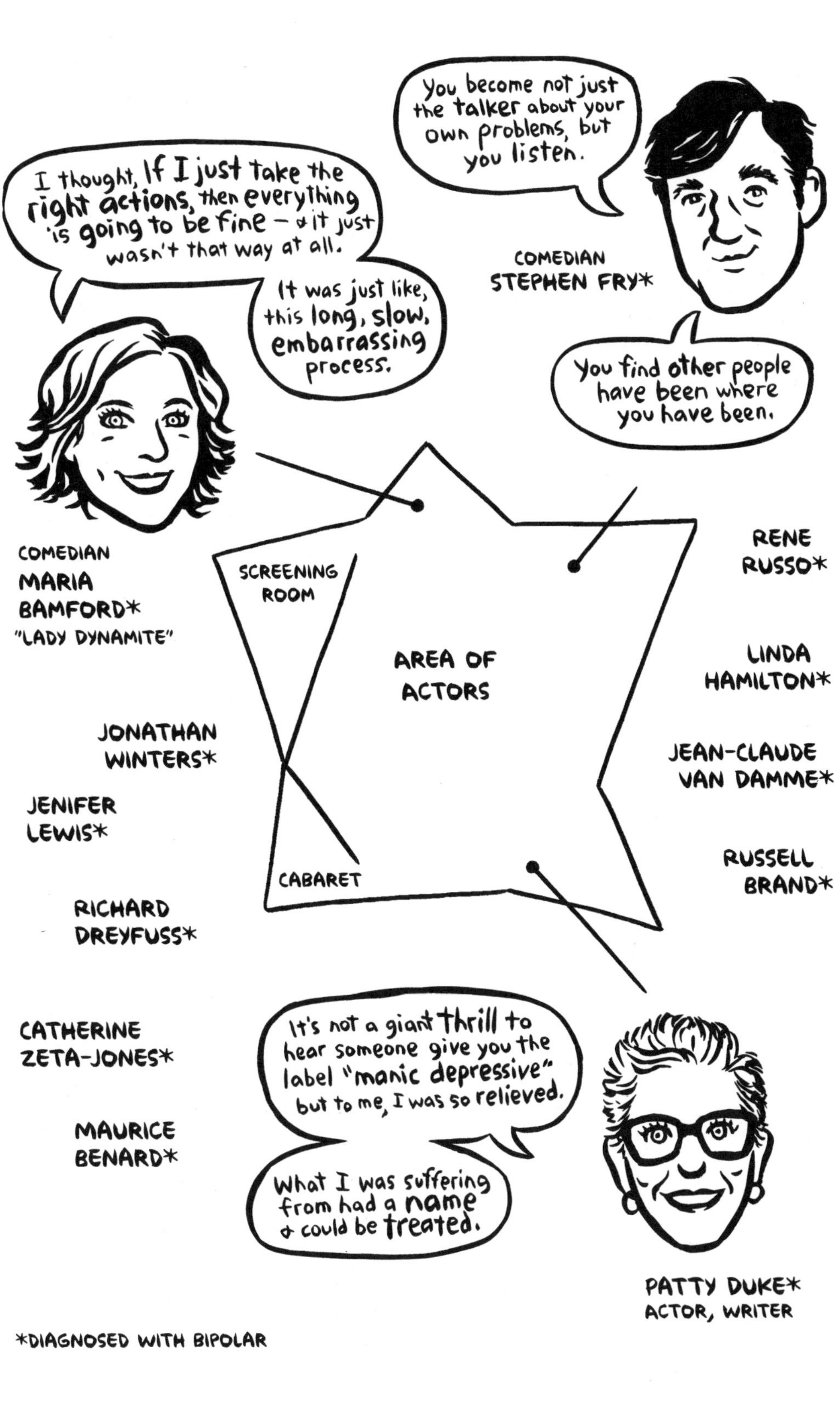
I thought, If I just take the right actions, then everything is going to be fine – & it just wasn't that way at all.
It was just like, this long, slow, embarrassing process.
COMEDIAN
MARIA BAMFORD*
"LADY DYNAMITE"
You become not just the talker about your own problems, but you listen.
COMEDIAN
STEPHEN FRY*
You find other people have been where you have been.
SCREENING ROOM
AREA OF ACTORS
CABARET
RENE RUSSO*
LINDA HAMILTON*
JEAN-CLAUDE VAN DAMME*
RUSSELL BRAND*
JONATHAN WINTERS*
JENIFER LEWIS*
RICHARD DREYFUSS*
CATHERINE ZETA-JONES*
MAURICE BENARD*
It's not a giant thrill to hear someone give you the label "manic depressive" but to me, I was so relieved.
What I was suffering from had a name & could be treated.
PATTY DUKE*
ACTOR, WRITER
*DIAGNOSED WITH BIPOLAR

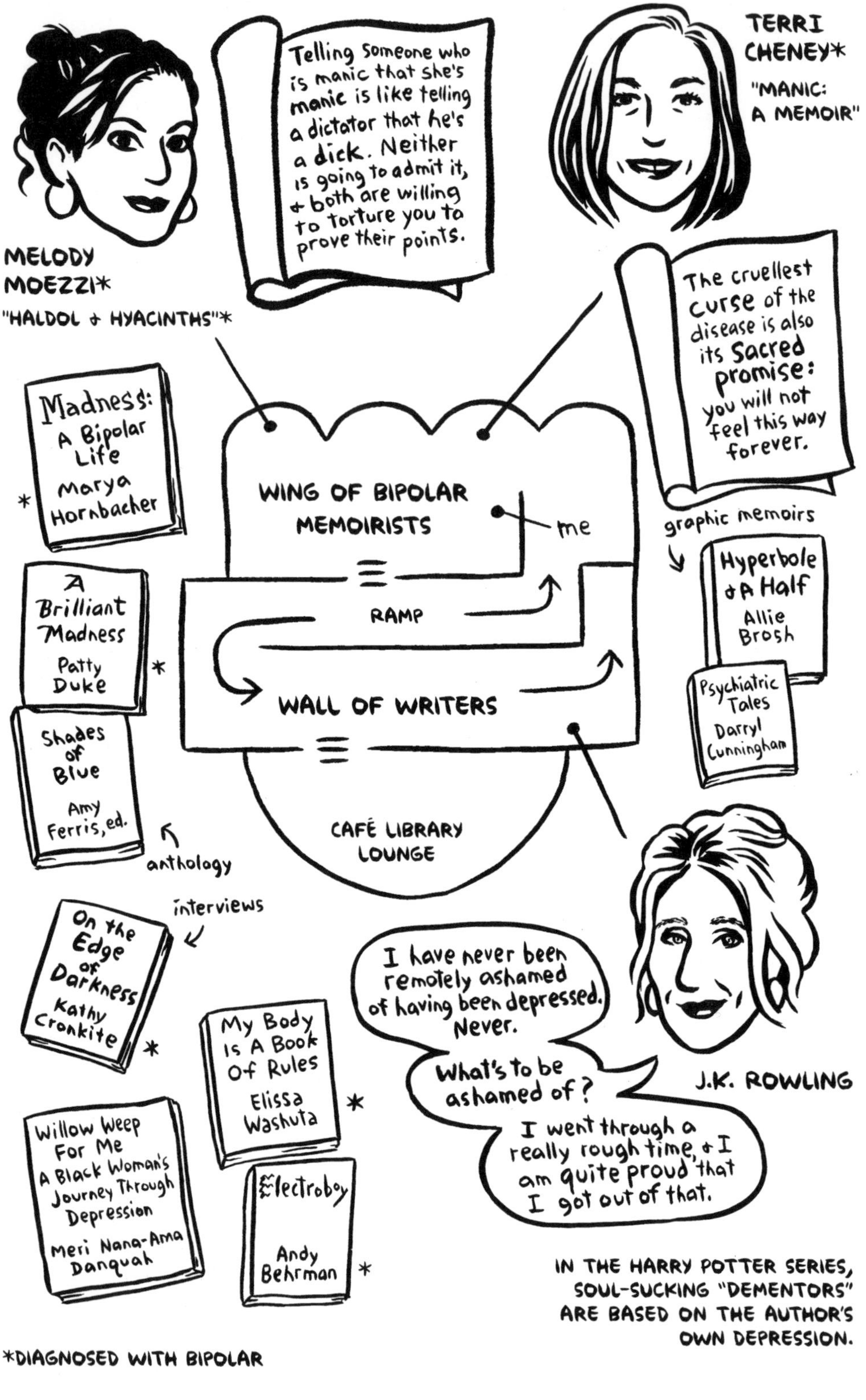
MELODY MOEZZI*
"HALDOL & HYACINTHS"*
Telling someone who is manic that she's manic is like telling a dictator that he's a dick. Neither is going to admit it, & both are willing to torture you to prove their points.
TERRI CHENEY*
"MANIC: A MEMOIR"
The cruellest curse of the disease is also its sacred promise: you will not feel this way forever.
WING OF BIPOLAR MEMOIRISTS
me
RAMP
WALL OF WRITERS
CAFÉ LIBRARY LOUNGE
Madness: A Bipolar Life Marya Hornbacher *
A Brilliant Madness Patty Duke *
Shades of Blue Amy Ferris, ed.
anthology
graphic memoirs
Hyperbole & A Half Allie Brosh
Psychiatric Tales Darryl Cunningham
interviews
On the Edge of Darkness Kathy Cronkite *
My Body Is A Book Of Rules Elissa Washuta *
Willow Weep For Me A Black Woman's Journey Through Depression Meri Nana-Ama Danquah
Electroboy Andy Behrman *
I have never been remotely ashamed of having been depressed. Never.
What's to be ashamed of?
I went through a really rough time, & I am quite proud that I got out of that.
J.K. ROWLING
IN THE HARRY POTTER SERIES, SOUL-SUCKING "DEMENTORS" ARE BASED ON THE AUTHOR'S OWN DEPRESSION.
*DIAGNOSED WITH BIPOLAR

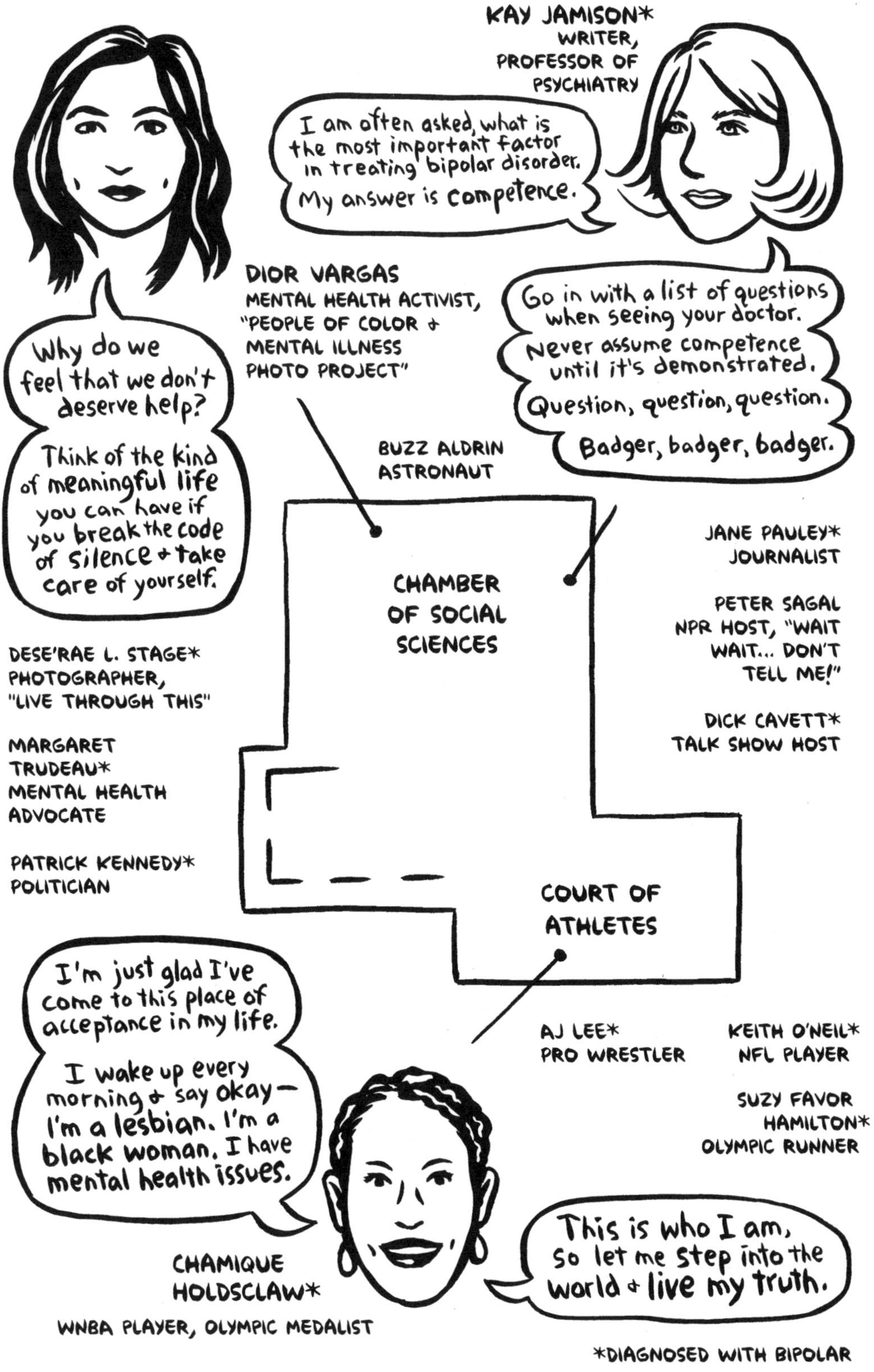
KAY JAMISON* WRITER, PROFESSOR OF PSYCHIATRY
I am often asked, what is the most important factor in treating bipolar disorder. My answer is competence.
Go in with a list of questions when seeing your doctor. Never assume competence until it's demonstrated. Question, question, question. Badger, badger, badger.
DIOR VARGAS MENTAL HEALTH ACTIVIST, "PEOPLE OF COLOR + MENTAL ILLNESS PHOTO PROJECT"
Why do we feel that we don't deserve help?
Think of the kind of meaningful life you can have if you break the code of silence + take care of yourself.
BUZZ ALDRIN ASTRONAUT
CHAMBER OF SOCIAL SCIENCES
JANE PAULEY* JOURNALIST
PETER SAGAL NPR HOST, "WAIT WAIT... DON'T TELL ME!"
DICK CAVETT* TALK SHOW HOST
DESE'RAE L. STAGE* PHOTOGRAPHER, "LIVE THROUGH THIS"
MARGARET TRUDEAU* MENTAL HEALTH ADVOCATE
PATRICK KENNEDY* POLITICIAN
COURT OF ATHLETES
AJ LEE* PRO WRESTLER
KEITH O'NEIL* NFL PLAYER
SUZY FAVOR HAMILTON* OLYMPIC RUNNER
I'm just glad I've come to this place of acceptance in my life.
I wake up every morning + say okay— I'm a lesbian. I'm a black woman. I have mental health issues.
This is who I am, so let me step into the world + live my truth.
CHAMIQUE HOLDSCLAW* WNBA PLAYER, OLYMPIC MEDALIST
*DIAGNOSED WITH BIPOLAR

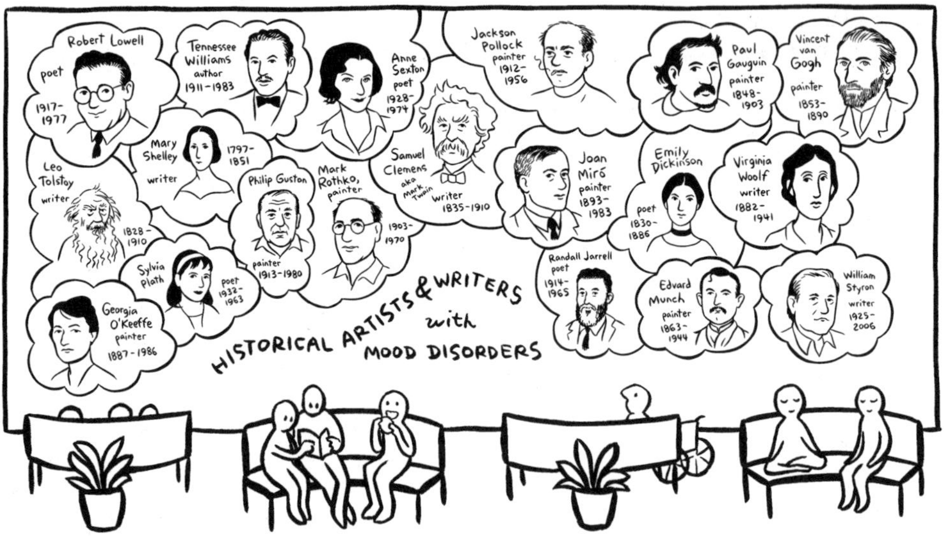
Robert Lowell
poet
1917-1977
Tennessee Williams
author
1911-1983
Anne Sexton
poet
1928-1974
Jackson Pollock
painter
1912-1956
Paul Gauguin
painter
1848-1903
Vincent van Gogh
painter
1853-1890
Mary Shelley
writer
1797-1851
Leo Tolstoy
writer
1828-1910
Philip Guston
painter
1913-1980
Mark Rothko,
painter
1903-1970
Samuel Clemens
aka Mark Twain
writer
1835-1910
Joan Miró
painter
1893-1983
Emily Dickinson
poet
1830-1886
Virginia Woolf
writer
1882-1941
Sylvia Plath
poet
1932-1963
Georgia O'Keeffe
painter
1887-1986
Randall Jarrell
poet
1914-1965
Edvard Munch
painter
1863-1944
William Styron
writer
1925-2006
HISTORICAL ARTISTS & WRITERS with MOOD DISORDERS

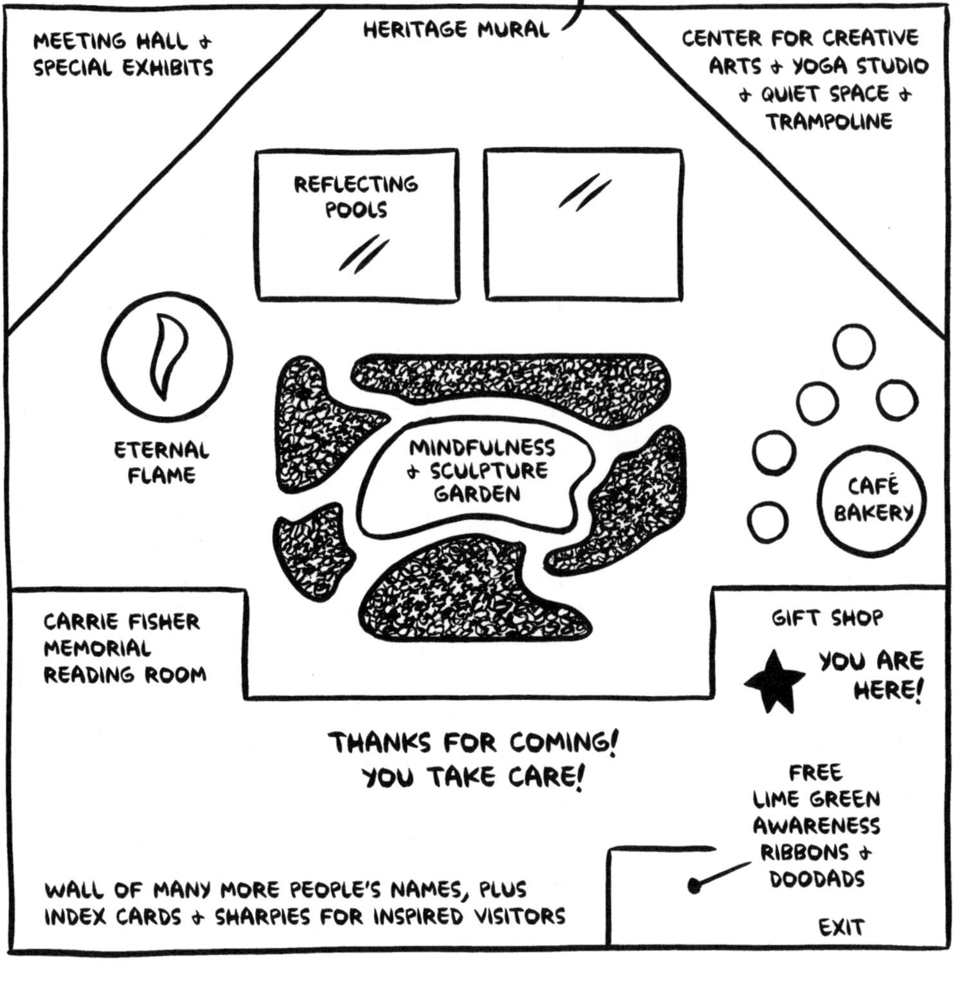
MEETING HALL & SPECIAL EXHIBITS
HERITAGE MURAL
CENTER FOR CREATIVE ARTS & YOGA STUDIO & QUIET SPACE & TRAMPOLINE
REFLECTING POOLS
ETERNAL FLAME
MINDFULNESS & SCULPTURE GARDEN
CAFÉ BAKERY
CARRIE FISHER MEMORIAL READING ROOM
GIFT SHOP
YOU ARE HERE!
THANKS FOR COMING! YOU TAKE CARE!
FREE LIME GREEN AWARENESS RIBBONS & DOODADS
WALL OF MANY MORE PEOPLE'S NAMES, PLUS INDEX CARDS & SHARPIES FOR INSPIRED VISITORS
EXIT

MOOD DISORDER HALL OF FAME GIFT SHOP!

PILLBOXES OF MANY SORTS!

SMEDMERTS

MARIA "The Bamfoo" BAMFORD

E-Z PE-Z TABLET DISPENSERS

WALLET INSERT

BEJEWELED ANTIQUE

Journals

EACH INCLUDES MOOD CHART TEMPLATES, INSPIRING QUOTES, & PLASTIC SLEEVES FOR MERIT BADGES

T-shirts
DESTIGMATIZE IN COMFORT!

CRAZY for LIFE

Crazylicious

NOBODY KNOWS I HAVE BIPOLAR

MY WHOLE FAMILY HAS ANXIETY & ALL I GOT WAS THIS LOUSY BIPOLAR DISORDER

MED ZEPPELIN

EVERY DAY IS MENTAL HEALTH AWARENESS DAY

ROCK STEADY

SMEDMERTS

FRONT

BACK

No-Mo Insomnia Moth

relax

release

THIS HEAD-BOBBING CUTIE PLAYS GUIDED SLEEP MEDITATIONS, WHITE NOISE, & BORING PODCASTS!

☆ ROCK STEADY ☆ Playlists

ROCK STEADY Mood Swing

STEADY Mood Swing

MANY HOURS FOR YOUR MANY MOODS

Sluggie

SUPER-SOFT BLANKET WITH DRAWSTRING COLLAR FOR NOSE & MOUTH. SUPREME COMFORT FOR A COCOON KIND OF DAY.

FOR DOCTORS!

SMEDMERTS
Prescription Pads

YOUR NAME, MD

Rx

SMEDMERTS!

...BECAUSE YOU KNOW PYCHOPHARMACOLOGICAL MONOTHERAPY ISN'T ENOUGH!

MERIT BADGES FOR BEING
OKAY WITH
WHO YOU ARE

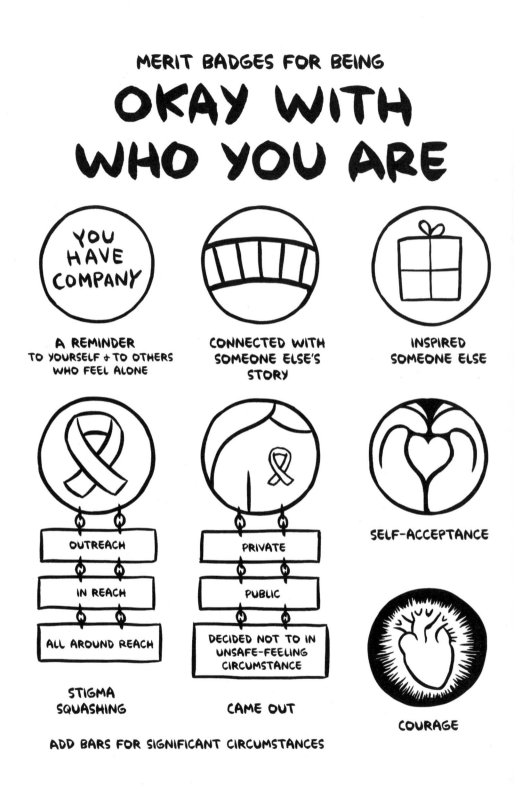

A REMINDER
TO YOURSELF & TO OTHERS
WHO FEEL ALONE

CONNECTED WITH
SOMEONE ELSE'S
STORY

INSPIRED
SOMEONE ELSE

YOU HAVE COMPANY

OUTREACH

IN REACH

ALL AROUND REACH

**STIGMA
SQUASHING**

PRIVATE

PUBLIC

DECIDED NOT TO IN
UNSAFE-FEELING
CIRCUMSTANCE

CAME OUT

SELF-ACCEPTANCE

COURAGE

ADD BARS FOR SIGNIFICANT CIRCUMSTANCES

CHAPTER 8
YOU ROCK

IT'S A TON OF STUFF TO DO & BE AWARE OF &
DEAL WITH. IT'S HARD. BIPOLAR DISORDER IS FOR
KEEPS, WHICH MEANS INCORPORATING YOUR VERSION
OF SMEDMERTS INTO THE REST OF YOUR LIFE.

I KNOW. I KNOW, I KNOW.

EXPECT THAT LIFE WILL ROCK YOU, BECAUSE IT WILL.
YOUR LIFE WILL HAVE RED FLAGPOLES BECAUSE THAT'S
WHAT LIFE DOES. YOU'LL HAVE RED FLAGS BECAUSE
THAT'S WHAT A MOOD DISORDER DOES.

ACCEPT & RESPECT THAT YOU NEED TO PRIORITIZE SLEEP (IN PARTICULAR) & TAKING YOUR MEDS (IF YOU TAKE MEDS).

MEET THE VAST ARRAY OF OBSTACLES WITH A VASTER ARRAY OF COPING TOOLS. MOST OF THE TIME, THERE ARE NO RIGHT ANSWERS. CHOOSE SOMETHING. IF IT DOESN'T WORK, TRY SOMETHING ELSE. MAKE SOMETHING UP. GIVE YOURSELF A TREAT FOR STICKING TO IT. EXPERIMENTING CAN BE FRUSTRATING. TRUST THAT YOU'LL GET THERE.

WHEN YOU'RE REALLY STRESSED OUT – WHEN THOSE RED FLAGS & FLAGPOLES COME AROUND, YOU MAY FEEL TOO BUSY TO EXERCISE OR DO YOUR MOOD CHART, OR WHATEVER YOU DO TO TAKE CARE OF YOURSELF. AS YOU MIGHT GUESS, THOSE ARE THE TIMES YOU ESPECIALLY NEED TO TAKE CARE OF YOURSELF.

WHAT DO YOU DO, THEN, IF THE DEMANDS ON YOUR TIME & ENERGY ARE TOO MUCH? IF BEING STRICT ABOUT YOUR ROUTINE KEEPS YOUR STRESS LEVEL DOWN, DO THAT. IF BEING FLEXIBLE ABOUT YOUR ROUTINE WORKS BETTER, DO THAT. TRY ONE. TRY THE OTHER. PRIORITIZE YOUR WELL-BEING, WHATEVER THAT MEANS.

IT'S IMPOSSIBLE TO HAVE A FLAWLESS, UNINTERRUPTED, 24/7 SELF-CARE ROUTINE. YOU MIGHT NOT HAVE TIME TO GET ENOUGH SLEEP AND EAT A GOOD BREAKFAST AND MEDITATE AND CATCH A 7AM FLIGHT. IT'S ABOUT BALANCE: CALIBRATE, RECALIBRATE. GET OFF SCHEDULE, GET BACK ON SCHEDULE. ROCK, STEADY.

FRUSTRATING BUT TRUE: MOST PEOPLE WITH BIPOLAR
DISORDER RELAPSE AT SOME POINT, EVEN WHEN WE'RE
TOTALLY IN LINE WITH TREATMENT. BUT EVEN IF YOU DO
SLIP ON YOUR TREATMENT PROGRAM & THEN RELAPSE, BE
KIND TO YOURSELF. LET GO OF GUILT, IT WON'T SERVE YOU.
HANG IN THERE. CALL YOUR DOCTOR. YOU GOT THIS.

KNOW THAT OPENING UP TO YOUR VULNERABILITY
IS STRENGTH. KNOW THAT REACHING OUT FOR
HELP IS STRENGTH.

KNOW THAT YOU DESERVE TO BE HEALTHY.

OKAY, MY LIKE-MINDED, MY TEAM...
BE WELL, BE BRAVE,
& DO YOUR THING.

ROCK STEADY --

ellen.

ACKNOWLEDGMENTS

ENORMOUS THANKS TO:

MY AGENT, HOLLY BEMISS; MY STAR EXPERT CONSULTANT, DR. ASHLEY BOUZIS; DR. TUSHAR KUMAR; HANA ABDI MOHAMED; & AHMED ALI OF SEATTLE'S SOMALI HEALTH BOARD.

THOSE WHO SHARED THEIR PERSONAL EXPERIENCES WITH ME, ESPECIALLY: ALLISON CONROY, NAMI SEATTLE'S IN OUR OWN VOICE SPEAKERS & BIPOLAR SUPPORT GROUP MEMBERS, & IN MEMORY OF AMY VANDERBECK.

SEAN HURLEY, JANE DAY, MARIA VANYO, KATE VRIJMOET, & MY COMICS & MEDICINE COLLEAGUES & COMMUNITY.

ALINA KIDO-MAZNER FOR RESEARCH ASSISTANCE, & RACHEL IVANOFF FOR PRODUCTION ASSISTANCE.

THE MACDOWELL COLONY FOR THE SUPPORT, TIME, & SPACE FOR ME TO SHAPE THE ENTIRE FIRST DRAFT, ATLANTIC CENTER FOR THE ARTS, & CENTRUM.

EVERYONE I MENTION IN ROCK STEADY, & EVERYONE & ALL THE STUFF THAT DIDN'T FIT, BECAUSE THERE'S SO MUCH THAT'S HELPFUL & INSPIRING – YOU WOULDN'T EVEN BELIEVE IT.

READERS, TEACHERS, THERAPISTS, & COUNSELORS WHO USE MARBLES IN THEIR WORK.

EVERYONE AT FANTAGRAPHICS BOOKS, ESPECIALLY GARY GROTH & ERIC REYNOLDS.

MY FAMILY, MY FRIENDS, & MY PSYCHIATRIST.

AND, OF COURSE: JACOB PETER FENNELL, MY STEADY, MY ROCK.

RESOURCES

ORGANIZATIONS

National Alliance for Mental Illness (NAMI)
nami.org
National organization focusing on mental health. Information, resources, advocacy, and more, with local and state chapters offering support groups and other services. Extensive and easy-to-navigate website.

Depression and Bipolar Support Alliance (DBSA)
dbsalliance.org
Peer-directed national organization focusing on depression and bipolar disorder. Information, resources, advocacy, and more, with local chapters offering support groups and other services.

Bring Change to Mind
Bringchange2mind.org
Nonprofit organization encouraging awareness of and dialogue about mental illness. Founded by actor Glenn Close after her sister was diagnosed with bipolar disorder.

SERVICES

National Suicide Prevention Lifeline
1-800-273-8255
suicidepreventionlifeline.org
Emotional support and crisis intervention hotline and chat. Also en Español (1-888-628-9454) and via TTY (1-800-799-4889).

Trans Lifeline
1-877-565-8860 (U.S.) or 1-877-330-6366 (Canada)
translifeline.org
Hotline for transgender people, staffed by transgender people.

The Trevor Project
1-866-488-7386
thetrevorproject.org
Crisis intervention and suicide prevention lifeline, chat, and text for LGBTQA+ youth.

Peer warmline
Warmline.org
Directory of non-crisis peer-run listening lines.

Now Matters Now
Nowmattersnow.org
Short videos with DBT techniques for coping with suicidal thoughts. Includes presentations by DBT founder Dr. Marsha Linehan.

INFORMATION & INSPIRATION

PubMed
Pubmed.gov
Free archive of biomedical studies and abstracts.

National Institute of Mental Health
nimh.nih.gov
Tons of information and resources.

PsyberGuide
psyberguide.org
Consumer guide for mental health apps and gadgets.

American Society of Addiction Medicine (ASAM)
asam.org
Primarily a professional website, which also includes educational information, patient resources, and provider locator for addiction specialists.

The Association of Black Psychologists (ABPsi)
abpsi.org
Primarily a professional website resource for Black/African-Centered Psychology, also includes resources, information, and publications.

Americans With Disabilities Act (ADA)
ada.gov
Information, resources, and technical assistance about disability rights issues.

BP Magazine
Bphope.com
Online and print magazine with news, features, and information by and for the bipolar community.

People of Color & Mental Illness Photo Project
diorvargas.com/poc-mental-illness/
Online crowd-sourced self-portrait project by Latina mental health activist, Dior Vargas. As of this printing, an ongoing project encouraging submissions.

BIBLIOGRAPHY

Abdullah MT & Brown TL. (2011, Aug). Mental Illness Stigma and Ethnocultural Beliefs, Values, and Norms: An Integrative Review. *Clinical Psychology Review*, 31(6), 934–948.

American Psychiatric Association. (2013). *Diagnostic and Statistical Manual of Mental Disorders* (5th ed.). Arlington, VA: American Psychiatric Publishing.

Amini, Adeel. (2008, March). Interview with J.K. Rowling. *The Student* magazine. Edinburgh, UK: Edinburgh University.

Australian Institute of Professional Counselors. (2014, June 16). Psychoeducation: Definition, Goals, and Methods. Retrieved January 3, 2108 from https://www.aipc.net.au/articles/psychoeducation-definition-goals-and-methods/.

Ayaki M, Hattori A, Maruyama Y, Nakano M, Yoshimura M, Kitazawa M, Negishi K, Tsubota K. Protective Effect of Blue-Light Shield Eyewear for Adults Against Light Pollution from Self-Luminous Devices Used at Night. *Chronobiology International*. Published online on 5 January 2016. doi: 10.3109/07420528.2015.1119158.

Beckett, L. (2014, June 10). Myth vs. Fact: Violence and Mental Health. *ProPublica*.

Bond K & Anderson I.M. (2015, June). Psychoeducation for Relapse Prevention in Bipolar Disorder: A Systematic Review of Efficacy in Randomized Controlled Trials. *Bipolar Disorders*, 17(4), 349–362. doi:10.1111/bdi.12287.

BP Magazine. (2017, March 1). Demi Lovato and "Be Vocal" release exciting new Documentary. Retrieved January 3, 2018, from https://www.bphope.com/hope-prepare-for-daylight-saving-time/.

BuzzFeedVideo. (2015, Dec 9). I Jumped Off the Golden Gate Bridge. Retrieved January 3, 2018, from https://www.youtube.com/watch?v=WcSUs9iZv-g.

Carey M, Jones K, Meadows G. (2014, June). Accuracy of General Practitioner Unassisted Detection of Depression. *Australian and New Zealand Journal of Psychiatry* 48: 571–578. doi: 10.1177/0004867413520047.

Chan, Yuan-Yu, et al. (2015, May). The Benefit of Combined Acupuncture and Antidepressant Medication for Depression: A Systematic Review and Meta-Analysis, *Journal of Affective Disorders,* Volume 176, 106–117.

Corrigan PW, Morris S, Larson J, Rafacz J, Wassel A, Michaels P, Wilkniss S, Batia K, Rüsch N. (2010, April). Self-Stigma and Coming Out About One's Mental Illness. *American Journal of Community Psychology*, 38(3), 259–275. doi: 10.1002/jcop.20363.

Cowles, C. (2016, Nov 11). How Can I Afford Mental Health Care? *New York Magazine*, TheCut.com.

Daigneault A, Duclos C, Saury S. (2015, March 15). Diagnosis of Bipolar Disorder in Primary and Secondary Care: What Have we Learned Over a 10-Year Period? *Journal of Affective Disorders* 174: 225–232. http://dx.doi.org/10.1016/j.jad.2014.10.057.

D'Arcangelo, L. (2016, Nov 28). Chamique Holdsclaw: Living Her Truth. *Curve Magazine*.

Dijk, S.V. (2009). *The Dialectical Behavior Therapy Skills Workbook for Bipolar Disorder: Using DBT to Regain Control of Your Emotions and Your Life*. Oakland, CA: New Harbinger.

Dimitrakopoulos S & Konstantakopoulos G. (2015, Jul–Sept). Pharmacological Agents Under Research for the Maintenance Treatment in Bipolar Disorder. *Psychiatriki*. 2015 Jul-Sep;26(3):169–80.

Federman, Russ & Thomson J. (2010). *Facing Bipolar: The Young Adult's Guide to Dealing with Bipolar Disorder*. Oakland, CA: New Harbinger Publications.

Fisher, Carrie. (2011). *Shockaholic*. New York, NY: Simon & Schuster.

Forney, Ellen. (2012). *Marbles: Mania, Depression, Michelangelo, & Me*. New York, NY: Avery.

Frank, E. (2007, May). Interpersonal and Social Rhythm Therapy: A Means of Improving Depression and preventing relapse in Bipolar Disorder. *Journal of Clinical Psychology*, 63(5), 463–473. doi:10.1002/jclp.20371.

Frank E, Swartz H & Boland E. (2007, Sept). An Intervention Addressing Rhythm Dysregulation in Bipolar Disorder. *Dialogues in Clinical Neuroscience*.

Fry, Stephen & Shanahan, William "Bill." (2017, April). Heads Together Campaign. Retrieved January 3, 2018 from https://www.youtube.com/watch?v=AHS7UtmQBpw&t=12s.

Geddes JR & Miklowitz DJ. (2013, May). Treatment of Bipolar Disorder. *The Lancet*, 381(9878), doi: 10.1016/S0140–6736(13)60857–0.

Gerston, Jill. (1987, Aug 12). A Star's Dark Life In Her New Book, Patty Duke Writes of a Stolen Identity, Suicide Attempts and Episodes of Anorexia and Alcohol Abuse. *Philadelphia Inquirer*.

Ghouse A.A., Sanches M., Zunta-Soares G., Swann A.C., Soares J.C. (2013). Overdiagnosis of Bipolar Disorder: A Critical Analysis of the Literature. *The Scientific World Journal*, 297087. doi: 10.1155/2013/297087.

Gilmartin, Paul. (2013, Jan 4). Interview with Maria Bamford. *Mental Illness Happy Hour* podcast [Episode 95]. Retrieved January 3, 2018, from http://mentalpod.com/Maria-Bamford-podcast.

Gooden, B.A. (1994, Jan–March). Mechanism of the Human Diving Response. *Integrative Physiological and Behavioral Science*, 29(1), 6-16. doi:10.1007/bf02691277.

Goodwin, Frederick & Kay Redfield Jamison. (2007). *Manic-Depressive Illness: Bipolar Disorders and Recurrent Depression*. Oxford, UK: Oxford University Press.

Grant, Sarah. (2015, March). Mary Lambert on Embracing Sanity, Remaking "Jessie's Girl" for Lesbians. *Rolling Stone*. Retrieved JANUARY 3, 2018 from https://www.rollingstone.com/music/features/mary-lambert-on-embracing-sanity-remaking-jessies-girl-for-lesbians-20150305.

Harfmann B.D., Schroder E.A., Esser K.A. (Epub 2014 Dec 15.) Circadian Rhythms, the Molecular Clock, and Skeletal Muscle. *Journal of Biological Rhythms*. 2015 Apr;30(2):84-94. doi: 10.1177/0748730414561638.

Harvey, A.G. (2008, July). Sleep and Circadian Rhythms in Bipolar Disorder: Seeking Synchrony, Harmony, and Regulation. *American Journal of Psychiatry*, 165(7), 820-829. doi:10.1176/appi.ajp.2008.08010098.

Hoyle, Staci, Elliott, Lydia & Comer, Linda. (2015, May). Available Screening Tools for Adults Suffering from Bipolar Affective Disorder in Primary Care: An Integrative Literature Review. *Journal of the American Association of Nurse Practitioners* Vol. 27. doi:10.1002/2327-6924.12214.

Jamison, Kay Redfield. (1995). *An Unquiet Mind: A Memoir of Moods and Madness*. New York, NY: Knopf.

Kid Cudi. (2016, Oct 4.) Facebook post. Retrieved January 3, 2018, from https://www.facebook.com/kidcudi/posts/10154706102758586.

Kildare, S. (2017, Jan 3). Routine Maintenance: Sticking to a Schedule Helps Maintain Balance for Bipolar. *BP Magazine*. Retrieved November 22, 2017, from https://www.bphope.com/routine-schedule-maintain-balance-bipolar/.

Logan, D.E. & Marlatt G.A. (2010, Feb). Harm Reduction Therapy: a Practice-Friendly Review of Research. *Journal of Clinical Psychology*. doi:10.1002/jclp.20669.

McInnis, Melvin G. Ask the Doctor: Bipolar, Sleep and Circadian Rhythms. *BP Magazine*. (2017, June 28). Retrieved November 22, 2017, from http://www.bphope.com/ask-the-doctor-bipolar-sleep-and-circadian-rhythms/.

McIntyre, Roger S. & Konarski, Jakub Z. (Epub 2010 Aug 23). Profiles of Atypical Antipsychotics in the Treatment of Bipolar Disorder. *The Journal of Clinical Psychiatry* 2005; 66 (suppl 3): 28–36. 11(17):2827-37. doi:10.1517/14656566.2010.510835.

Melo M.C., Daher E.D., Albuquerque S.G., & Bruin V.M. (2016, July). Exercise in Bipolar Patients: A Systematic Review. *Journal of Affective Disorders*, 198, 32–38. doi:10.1016/j.jad.2016.03.004.

Moezzi, Melody. (2016, Oct 4). Maria Bamford Turns Bipolar into Funny Business. *BP Magazine*. Retrieved January 3, 2018, from https://www.bphope.com/maria-bamford-turns-bipolar-into-funny-business/.

Morris, Chad D., David J. Miklowitz, and Jeanette A. Waxmonsky (2007, May). Family-Focused Treatment for Bipolar Disorder in Adults and Youth. *The Journal of Clinical Psychology*; 63(5): 433–445. doi: 10.1002/jclp.20359.

Najafi-Vosough R, Ghaleiham A, Faradmal J, Mahjub H. (2016, July). Recurrence in Patients with Bipolar Disorder and its Risk Factors. *The Iranian Journal of Psychiatry* 2016; 11: 173-177.

Navara K.J. & Nelson R.J. (2007, Oct). The Dark Side of Light at Night: Physiological, Epidemiological, and Ecological Consequences. *Journal of Pineal Research*, 43(3), 215-224. doi:10.1111/j.1600-079x.2007.00473.x.

Norton, Amy. (2009, Aug 13). Some Conditions Misdiagnosed as Bipolar Disorder. Reuters, Health News. Retrieved January 3, 2018, from https://www.reuters.com/article/us-misdiagnosed-bipolar/some-conditions-misdiagnosed-as-bipolar-disorder-idUSTRE57C4SZ20090813.

Portugal E.M., Cevada T., Monteiro-Junior R.S., Guimarães T.T., Rubini E.D., Lattari E., . . . Deslandes A.C. (2013). Neuroscience of Exercise: From Neurobiology Mechanisms to Mental Health. *Neuropsychobiology*, 68(1), 1–14. doi:10.1159/000350946.

President's New Freedom Commission on Mental Health. (n.d.). Retrieved November 22, 2017, from http://govinfo.library.unt.edu/mentalhealthcommission/reports/FinalReport/FullReport-02.htm.

Roberts, Michelle (2009, Nov 1). Dual Diagnosis of Bipolar & Substance Abuse. *BP Magazine*. Retrieved November 22, 2017, from https://www.bphope.com/walking-the-line-with-dual-diagnosis/.

Roberts, Michelle. (2009, Aug 1). Hospitalization: Setback or Reset? *BP Magazine*. Retrieved January 3, 2018, from https://www.bphope.com/hospitalization-setback-or-reset/.

Ruriani, Alyse. (2015, Nov 23). What It's Like Going to the Emergency Room for Suicidal Thoughts. *The Mighty*. Retrieved January 3, 2018 from https://themighty.com/2015/11/what-its-like-going-to-the-emergency-room-for-suicidal-thoughts/.

Sakugawa, Yumi. (2015). *There is No Right Way to Meditate: And Other Lessons*. New York, NY: Adams Media.

Saladin M.E., & Ana E.J. (2004, May). Controlled Drinking: More Than Just a Controversy. *Current Opinion in Psychiatry*, 17(3), 175-187. doi:10.1097/00001504-200405000-00005.

Salmon, Jacquelene. (2009, Feb 1). Kay Redfield Jamison: A Profile in Courage. *BP Magazine*. Retrieved January 3, 2018, from https://www.bphope.com/kay-redfield-jamison-a-profile-in-courage/.

Särkämö T, Tervaniemi, M, Huotilainen M. (2014, July). Music Perception and Cognition: Development, Neural Basis, and Rehabilitative Use of Music. *Wiley Interdisciplinary Reviews: Cognitive Science*. 2013 Jul;4(4):441-51. doi: 10.1002/wcs.1237.

Savage, Dan. (2014). *American Savage: Insights, Slights, and Fights on Faith, Sex, Love, and Politics*. New York, NY: Penguin.

Schibler, Ueli, & Sassone-Corsi, Paolo. (2002, Dec). A Web of Circadian Pacemakers. *Cell*, Volume 111, Issue 7, p. 919–922, 27.

Schuster, S. (2016, Jan 20). 23 Messages for Anyone Considering Suicide, From People Who've Been There. *The Mighty*. Retrieved November 22, 2017, from https://themighty.com/2016/01/advice-for-anyone-considering-suicide/.

Sledge, W.H., Lawless, M., Sells, D., Wieland, M., O'Connell, M., & Davidson, L. (2011, May). Effectiveness of Peer Support in Reducing Readmissions of Persons With Multiple Psychiatric Hospitalizations. *Psychiatric Services*, 62(5), 541. doi:10.1176/appi.ps.62.5.541.

Stage, Dese'Rae L. *Live Through This*. (2010–ongoing). Livethroughthis.org.

Stuart, H. (2016, May 10). Reducing the Stigma of Mental Illness. *Global Mental Health*, 3, e17. doi: 10.1017/gmh.2016.11.

Suicide Prevention. (2017, Sept 15). Retrieved November 22, 2017, from https://www.samhsa.gov/suicide-prevention.

Szentagotai, A., & David, D. (2010, Jan). The Efficacy of Cognitive-Behavioral Therapy in Bipolar Disorder: A Quantitative Meta-Analysis. *The Journal of Clinical Psychiatry*, 71(01), 66–72. doi:10.4088/jcp.08r04559yel.

Tan, Zhai Yun. (2016, Aug 29). Depression Treatment Often Doesn't Go to Those Most in Need. *NPR Shots*. Retrieved January 3, 2018 from https://www.npr.org/sections/health-shots/2016/08/29/491819007/screening-positive-for-depression-doesn-t-mean-you-ll-get-treatment-study-finds.

Tarsy D., Lungu C., Baldessarini R.J. (2011). Epidemiology of Tardive Dyskinesia Before and During the Era of Modern Antipsychotic Drugs. *Handbook Clinical Neurology*. 2011;100:601-16. doi: 10.1016/B978-0-444-52014-2.00043-4.

Taylor, Whit. (2015, March 8). The Myth of the Strong Black Woman. TheNib.com.

Todd, Douglas. (2014, Oct 25). Tackling the Stigma of Mental Illness Among Asian Men. *Vancouver Sun*.

Vargas, Dior. (2017, April.) The most important thing I've learned about depression is to just keep going, no matter how hard it seems. OptionB.org.

Walker G, Bryant W. (2013). Peer Support in Adult Mental Health Services: A Metasynthesis of Qualitative Findings. *Psychiatric Rehabilitation Journal* 2013; 36(1): 28–34.

White, Ruth (2014). *Preventing Bipolar Relapse*. Oakland, CA: New Harbinger Publications.

Williams J.M.G., Alatiq Y., Crane C., Barnhofer T., Fennell M. J. V., Duggan D.S., et al. Goodwin G.M. (2008, April). Mindfulness-Based Cognitive Therapy (MBCT) in Bipolar Disorder: Preliminary Evaluation of Immediate Effects on Between Episode Functioning. *Journal of Affective Disorders*, 107, 275–279. doi: 10.1016/j.jad.2007.08.022.

INDEX